Pancreatitis Cookbook

The Ultimate Pancreatitis Guide with More Than 120 Easy & Delicious Pancreatitis Diet Recipes to Improve Your Enzymes and Health. 21 Day Pancreatic Meal Plan Included.

Author: Sophia Wilson

The trademarks that are used are without any consent, and the publication of the trademark is without permission or backing by the trademark owner. All trademarks and brands within this book are for clarifying purposes only and are the owned by the owners themselves, not affiliated with this document.

Table of Contents

What are the Symptoms of Your Pancreas Not Working Properly?

When your pancreas becomes inflamed or begins to break down you will experience discomfort to different degrees with a myriad of symptoms. Some symptoms may disappear without treatment, but severe cases can cause life-threatening complications.

Acute pancreatitis attacks typically happens as a result of gallstones from the gallbladder obstructing the pancreatic duct. The signs to look out for are:
- abdominal pain
- nausea
- fever
- vomiting.

Chronic pancreatitis occurs after repeated bouts of acute inflammation that progressively destroy the gland cells over time. Its symptoms are:
- greasy and smelly feces
- unintended weight loss
- intense abdominal pain

NOTE: If you have any of these symptoms, talk to a physician immediately.

Other Possible Pancreas Related Diseases

Diabetes

Diabetes is a serious long-term disease that alters how your body deals with the glucose found in your blood. Glucose is a type of sugar that is always present in the human blood. So, when the condition arises, there is always glucose to react to. There are type 1 and type 2 Diabetes, but the majority of the people who have Diabetes have the type 2. In the U.S. alone, around 27 million people live with this condition. There are some other 86 million people who have prediabetes, a condition just short of diabetes. In this case, their blood glucose is too high to be normal, but also too low to be fully diabetic yet.

Part of the job of your pancreas is to produce a hormone known as insulin. This insulin is the hormone what allows your cells to be able to convert the glucose found in your food into energy. People who live with type 2 diabetes still produce insulin. However, the changes in the cells have made them unable to fully utilize it as they normally should. This is what doctors call insulin resistance.

At the initial stage, the pancreas frantically tries producing more insulin to compensate for shortage of glucose in the cells. At a point, the work overload couldn't be maintained. This is when the sugar starts accumulating in your blood instead.

Pancreatic Cancer

Pancreatic cancer, put simply, is the presence of one or more cancerous masses or tumors that develop within the cells of the pancreas.

Allowed Nutrition & Foods to Avoid for Pancreatic Health

As stated, above patients diagnosed with chronic pancreatitis are required to make specific diet and lifestyle changes to help boost the health of the pancreas and to aid in preventing future pancreatitis attacks.

The most important tip you will need to employ is to avoid the foods that can lead to further inflammation. These include:

- mayonnaise

- deep fried foods

- organ meats

- Sugar filled desserts

- full-fat dairy

- red meat

- heavily processed snacks

- most fast food meals

- full fat margarine and butter

- Sugar filled beverages

Lifestyle & Diet Changes When Recovering From Pancreatitis

Please Note: Patients with acute pancreatitis are advised to visit your medical professional or emergency department of your hospital as these patients are typically admitted for up to a week and taken of ALL foods. During this time, their bodies are provided nutrients via IV fluids and pain killers are supplied to assist with the associated symptoms. After release, most patients you generally are allowed to go back to enjoying their usual balanced diet.

Okay, now that we have gotten that out of the way, while working with your medical professional to combat chronic pancreatitis long term, you should:

- avoid drinking alcohol,
- ensure you get the recommended dosage of water or electrolyte beverage daily,
- consult your physician about required supplements or vitamins to assist the decreased functionalities of the pancreas.
- quit smoking, if you are a smoker, and
- switch your diet to one that is moderately high in protein, and low in fat that won't further inflame or damage your pancreas.

How to: Pancreas Attacks

Now that we have explored a general overview of the pancreas and pancreatitis, let's address the question on most patient's minds. Is there anything that can be done to prevent repeated attacks of acute pancreatitis?

This would depend largely on the cause of pancreatitis in that person in the first place. So, you will need to work along with a medical professional to pinpoint all the causes that could cost an inflammation increase. This is because there are some causes that once treated you could prevent other attacks. A good example of this pancreatitis caused by gallstones in a patient with a lipid issue. If the physician finds that they were caused solely by the medication they use to treat the underlying lipid issue or an excess of alcohol use, they could easily limit the likelihood of another pancreatitis attack by possibly replacing that medication or avoiding alcohol.

If no definite cause can be found, however, prevention becomes a tad tricky. There have been studies, at least in adults, that looked at different treatment regimens to see if acute or chronic pancreatitis could be less frequent. They analyzed if the pain experienced could be in between attacks or if things like pancreatic enzyme supplementation or antioxidant cocktails could be used. They also explored if following a low-fat diet only was indeed the way to go.

The results confirmed what was already suspected to be true, and that was that following a low-fat diet that is also moderately high in protein can aid in improving the health of the pancreas and, in turn, successfully lessening future pancreatitis attacks in patients of all ages. There haven't been any specific medication that has been proven to fully prevent all attacks, however, it is recommended that you try to incorporate regular exercise into your lifestyle and that you work along with your doctor to come up with possible pain medication and other treatments to reduce or prevent inflammation in the pancreas.

Okay, now that you have gathered a better understanding of what pancreatitis is, and how to go about better caring for your pancreas. Let's dive into our sample meal plan and delicious pancreatitis diet recipes to improve your enzymes and health.

Sample 21 Day 21 Day Pancreatic Meal Plan

Day	Breakfast	Lunch	Dinner
1	Cheese & Bacon Muffins	Pan-Smoked Spiced Chicken Breasts with Fruit Salsa	Salmon & Broccoli
2	Cheese & Bacon Muffins	Simple Mexican Taco Wings	Salmon & Broccoli
3	Soft Boiled Egg and Asparagus	Pan-Smoked Spiced Chicken Breasts with Fruit Salsa	Pork Casserole
4	Crustless Spinach Quiche	Sweet Potato & Collard Hash	Pork Casserole
5	Crustless Spinach Quiche	Chicken Zoodle Soup	Balsamic Roast Pork
6	Italian Baked Eggs	Chipotle Pork Canitas	Balsamic Roast Pork
7	Baked Eggs with Tomato and Spinach	Sweet Potato & Collard Hash	Duck Confit
8	Cauliflower Quiche	Pan-Smoked Spiced Chicken Breasts with Fruit Salsa	Chicken 2-Ways
9	Baked Eggs with Tomato and Spinach	Cajun Greens	Chicken 2-Ways
10	Egg Cups	Simple Mexican Taco Wings	Baked Fish with Tomatoes and Mushrooms
11	Cauliflower Quiche	Tasty Shredded Chicken	Baked Fish with Tomatoes and Mushrooms
12	Soft Boiled Egg and Asparagus	Tasty Shredded Chicken	Lamb Leg
13	Cheese & Bacon Muffins	Sweet Potato & Collard Hash	Lamb Leg
14	Cheese & Bacon Muffins	Chicken Souvlaki Kebobs	Flounder in Stewed Tomatoes
15	Italian Baked Eggs	Easy Fisherman's Stew	Flounder in Stewed Tomatoes
16	Cauliflower Quiche	Chicken Zoodle Soup	30-Minute Fall-Off

			The-Bone Chicken
17	Cauliflower Quiche	Pork Egg Roll Soup	Baked Fish with Tomatoes and Mushrooms
18	Italian Baked Eggs	Tasty Shredded Chicken	Balsamic Roast Pork
19	Soft Boiled Egg and Asparagus	Sweet Potato & Collard Hash	Balsamic Roast Pork
20	Crustless Spinach Quiche	Simple Mexican Taco Wings	Chicken 2-Ways
21	Crustless Spinach Quiche	Pan-Smoked Spiced Chicken Breasts with Fruit Salsa	Chicken 2-Ways

Breakfast

1. Cheese & Bacon Muffins

Servings|4   Prep. Time|15 minutes   Cook Time|20 minutes
Nutritional Content (per serving):
Cal|127   Fat|9.4g   Protein|9.7g   Carbs|0.9g

Ingredients:

1 green onion, diced
1/4 teaspoon lemon pepper seasoning
4 eggs

4 slices bacon (grass-fed), cooked & crumbled
4 tablespoons low fat parmesan cheese, shredded

Directions:

1. Set your oven to preheat to 400 degrees F. Break the eggs into a measuring bowl, preferably large with a pout. Add the seasoning; beat well.
2. Divide the bacon, parmesan, and green onion between the muffin cups. Pour the egg mixture into the cups.
3. Set your muffin tray to bake for 15 – 20 minutes or until fully cooked.
4. Remove the tray from the oven. Serve. Refrigerate leftovers for 1 week. Microwave on HIGH for 30 seconds to reheat.

2. Soft Boiled Egg and Asparagus

Servings| 2 Prep. Time|5 minutes   Cook Time|10 minutes
Nutritional Content (per serving):
Cal| 90   Fat|5g   Protein|9g   Carbs|4g

Ingredients:

Egg (1 large)
Asparagus (5 long, peeled, trimmed)

Salt and pepper (to taste)

Directions:

1. Set a large saucepan with salted water over high heat and allow to come to a boil. Add the asparagus and cook until fork tender (about 5 min).
2. Add your egg to the saucepan at the same time and allow to cook for 3 minutes.

3. Set an egg cup with egg on a servings plate and serve alongside asparagus, salt, and pepper.

3. *Crustless Spinach Quiche*

Servings|6   Prep. Time|15 minutes   Cook Time|20 minutes
Nutritional Content (per serving):
Cal|127   Fat|9g   Protein|10g   Carbs|5g

Ingredients:

1 1/2 cup water, for the IP

1 cup preferred mushrooms

1/2 cup coconut milk

1/2 teaspoon salt

1/4 cup low fat parmesan cheese, shredded

1/4 teaspoon black pepper (fresh ground)

12 eggs (large)

3 cups baby spinach (fresh), roughly chopped

3 green onions (large), sliced

Directions:

1. Put the IP trivet and pour the water into the inner pot. In a bowl, preferably large, whisk the eggs, milk, salt, and pepper. Add the spinach, preferred veggies, and green onions in the baking dish; stir to mix well.

2. Put the dish on the trivet. Lock the lid and close the pressure valve. Set to HIGH pressure for 20 minutes. When the timer beeps, press CANCEL, NPR for 10 minutes, QPR, and open the lid. Remove the dish from the pot. If preferred, broil the quiche till the top is light brown.

4. Sweet Potato and Egg Skillet

Servings|2   Prep. Time|10 minutes   Cook Time|13 minutes
Nutritional Content (per serving):
Cal|216   Fat|11 g   Protein|16g   Carbs|13g

Ingredients:

1 large sweet potato

4 large eggs

1/2 teaspoon smoked paprika (or any seasoning of your choice)

pinch of pepper and salt, to taste

Directions:

1. Set the broiler to high heat. Pierce the sweet potato all over with a fork. Broil until tender.
2. Remove from broiler and cool slightly. Place one oven rack on the broiler's highest or second highest level. Once cooled, slice the sweet potatoes into thin ¼-inch rounds.
3. Lightly grease a skillet. Arrange the sweet potatoes in the skillet in a single flat layer. Beat the eggs and pour them evenly over the sweet potatoes.
4. Sprinkle with pepper, salt and paprika. Place the entire skillet in the broiler and cook for 3 minutes until the top turns golden brown and the eggs have set. Serve while still hot.

5. *Italian Baked Eggs*

Servings|4   Prep. Time|10 minutes   Cook Time|25 minutes
Nutritional Content (per serving):
Cal|240   Fat|13 g   Protein|14g   Carbs|7g

Ingredients:

½ pint grape tomatoes

1 red or orange bell pepper, cored and cut into slices

¼ red onion, diced

2 cloves of garlic, roughly chopped

2 tablespoons extra virgin olive oil

⅛ teaspoon salt

¼ teaspoon freshly ground

black pepper

½ cup tomato sauce

6 eggs

¼ cup low fat mozzarella cheese, shredded

2 tablespoons pecorino cheese

Directions:

1. Set your oven to preheat to 475°F. Toss onion, grape tomatoes, pepper, and garlic with olive oil. Season with salt and pepper.
2. Bake in oven for 15 minutes or when your tomatoes start to burst. Remove vegetables from oven. Pour tomato sauce into dish and stir.
3. Pour eggs over top of the vegetable mixture. Top with low fat mozzarella cheese and return to oven.
4. Bake 10 minutes or when your whites are no longer translucent. Remove from oven and sprinkle with pecorino cheese. Serve immediately.

6. Cauliflower Quiche

Servings|4   Prep. Time|20 minutes   Cook Time|35 minutes
Nutritional Content (per serving):
Cal|176   Fat|5 g   Protein|17g   Carbs|8 g

Ingredients:

½ head cauliflower, chopped

½ cup almond milk

4 eggs

2 cloves garlic, minced

1 tablespoon olive oil

½ teaspoon salt

1 cup baby spinach

1 cup pitted olives, chopped or sliced

3 cups water

Directions:

1. Set your oven to preheat to 350 degrees F. Make sure you steam the cauliflower first. Pour a cup of water over the cauliflower into a pot. Then cover and place on medium heat to steam.
2. In a bowl, whisk your eggs with almond milk, baby spinach and salt.
3. Combine with steamed cauliflower. Use 4 ramekins to distribute the mixture you have made. Place ramekins into a hotel pan and pour the remaining 3 cups of water around them. Cover the hotel pan with tin foil.
4. Set to steam in your preheated oven for 30 – 35 minutes or until fully cooked. Serve with olives.

7. *Roasted Superfood Vegetables Frittata*

Servings|6   Prep. Time|20 minutes   Cook Time|1 hr. 15 minutes
Nutritional Content (per serving):
Cal|139   Fat|7 g   Protein|31 g   Carbs|18 g

Ingredients:

3 medium red bell peppers, remove and discard seeds, slice into quarters
Nonstick cooking spray
1 medium onion, sliced into 1/2-inch slices
4 cloves garlic, keep unpeeled

2 large zucchini, sliced into 3-1/2-inch strips
1 tablespoon olive oil
1 teaspoon salt
1/4 cup fresh parsley, chopped
4 eggs plus 6 egg whites
1/4 teaspoon cayenne pepper

Directions:

1. Prepare the oven to 425F. Arrange the oven racks so that one is at the lowest position and another is in the middle. Take 2 baking pans with shallow bottoms. Line with foil. Spray the surface lightly with cooking spray. Put garlic and bell pepper in one of the prepared baking pans.
2. Place onions and zucchini in the other pan. Spray the vegetables lightly with some of the cooking spray. Place the pan with the onions and zucchini on the lower oven rack.
3. Place the other pan on the center oven rack. Roast the vegetables for 15 minutes. Remove the pans and change the positions on the oven. Place the pan with the onions-zucchini on the center rack and the other pan on the lower rack. Roast for another 10 minutes, until the vegetables are charred.
4. Remove the pans from the oven and set aside for 5 minutes. Lower the oven temperature to 350 F. Remove the skins from garlic and peppers. Chop everything coarsely. Put in a mixing bowl.
5. Add ½ teaspoon salt and parsley. Mix. Lightly grease the bottom of a 9-inch round baking pan.
6. Put eggs and egg whites in a mixing bowl, season with the remaining salt and the cayenne pepper, and then whisk thoroughly.
7. Pour the egg mixture over the vegetables. Pour the entire mixture into the prepared round pan. Bake in 350-degree oven for 45 to 50 minutes. Once the center has set, remove the frittata from the oven. Let the frittata rest for about 5 minutes so it can set. Slice and serve while still warm.

8. Baked Eggs with Tomato and Spinach

Servings|4   Prep. Time|5 minutes   Cook Time|15 minutes
Nutritional Content (per serving):
Cal|114   Fat|7 g   Protein|29 g   Carbs|13g

Ingredients:

1 can (400g) tomatoes, chopped	4 eggs
1 bag (100g) spinach	1 tsp chili flakes

Directions:

1. Heat the oven to 200°C. Place spinach in a colander. Pour boiling water over the leaves to wilt them. Squeeze out the spinach's excess water and divide the vegetables among 4 small dishes (ovenproof).
2. Mix the tomatoes with some seasoning and the chili flakes. Add to the spinach. In each dish, make a well in the center, and crack open an egg.
3. Bake for about 12 to 15 minutes. You may even bake the eggs longer, depending on your eggs' doneness. If desired, serve with crusty bread.

9. Artichoke Spinach Quiche Cup

Servings|3   Prep. Time|15 minutes   Cook Time|15 minutes
Nutritional Content (per serving):
Cal|325   Fat|13 g   Protein|25g   Carbs|18g

Ingredients:

1 14.5-ounce can artichoke hearts, drained and chopped	5 eggs, lightly whisked
	2 cloves garlic, minced
1 package frozen spinach, thawed and drained	1/2 cup chopped white onion
	1/4 teaspoon pepper
2/3 cup almond milk	1/4 teaspoon salt

Directions:

1. Prepare the oven to 350F. Line 12 baking cups with cupcake liners. Place all the listed ingredients in a large mixing bowl. Stir into a well-combined batter. Scoop batter into prepared baking cups, filling each until nearly full. Bake the quiche. Check if the filling is done.
2. Insert a toothpick in the center of the quiche and it should come out clean. Remove the quiche from the oven and serve while still hot.

10. *Egg Cups*

Servings|6   Prep. Time|45 minutes   Cook Time|12 minutes
Nutritional Content (per serving):
Cal|289   Fat|9 g   Protein|21g   Carbs|9g

Ingredients:

1 yellow onion

3 cups shiitake mushrooms

2 leaves kale

2 cloves garlic

1 tsp turmeric

1/2 tsp dried thyme

1/2 tsp oregano

1 tsp salt

1 tsp freshly ground pepper

1 Tbs olive oil

10 eggs

1/2 cup nutritional yeast

Directions:

1. Finely chop onion, mushrooms, and kale. Peel and press or mince garlic. Sauté oregano, onion, turmeric, garlic, thyme, salt, and pepper and olive oil over medium heat until onions begin to soften, and spices are fragrant.

2. Add mushrooms and kale, and continue to cook, stirring frequently, until the kale is bright green. Distribute mushroom mixture to ten muffin tins. Crack an egg into each tin. Distribute nutritional yeast among the tins. Bake for twelve minutes at 400 degrees. Allow to set for a few minutes before serving. Enjoy

11. *Baked Eggs with Tomato and Spinach*

Servings|4   Prep. Time|5 minutes   Cook Time|15 minutes
Nutritional Content (per serving):
Cal|114   Fat|7 g   Protein|9g   Carbs|3g

Ingredients

1 can (400g) tomatoes, chopped   4 eggs
1 bag (100g) spinach   1 tsp chili flakes

Directions

1. Heat the oven to 200°C. Place spinach in a colander. Pour boiling water over the leaves to wilt them. Squeeze out the spinach's excess water and divide the vegetables among 4 small dishes (ovenproof).
2. Mix the tomatoes with some seasoning and the chili flakes. Add to the spinach. In each dish, make a well in the center, and crack open an egg. Bake for about 12 to 15 minutes. You may even bake the eggs longer, depending on your eggs' doneness. If desired, serve with crusty bread.

12. *Spinach Omelet*

Servings|1   Prep. Time|5 minutes   Cook Time|5 minutes
Nutritional Content (per serving):
Cal|161   Fat|10 g   Protein|13g   Carbs|6g

Ingredients:

Eggs (2)   Salt and pepper (to taste)
spinach leaves (60 grams)

Directions:

1. Add your eggs and spinach together in a medium bowl, season with salt, and pepper and whisk to combine. Set a lightly greased skillet over medium heat and allow to get hot.
2. Add egg mixture, once hot, and cook until egg begins to set (about 3 min). Flip your egg over halfway to form an omelet and continue to cook until fully set (about another 2 mins). Enjoy!

13. *Spinach and Egg Bites*

Servings|4   Prep. Time|45 minutes   Cook Time|12 minutes
Nutritional Content (per serving):
Cal|412   Fat|8 g   Protein|29g   Carbs|34g

Ingredients

1 cup spinach, roughly chopped.

2 cups shitake mushrooms, chopped

1/3 cup green onions, chopped

1 large clove garlic, peeled and pressed

1/2 cup uncooked millet

2 cups water

6 eggs

1 cup coconut milk

1/2 tsp salt

1/2 tsp pepper

1/2 cup nutritional yeast

1 tsp turmeric

Directions

1. Set the oven to preheat to 350 degrees F. Lightly grease your muffin tin. Toast millet over medium heat, stirring occasionally.

2. Add water and salt and water, cover, and switch to high heat allowing to boil heat to boil. Reduce heat slightly and continue to cook until water is absorbed. In a medium bowl, whisk eggs, coconut milk, salt, pepper, turmeric, and garlic.

3. Toss together with millet, spinach, mushrooms, and green onions; mix very well. Spoon into muffin cups; bake ten to twelve minutes, or until lightly firm to the touch. Sprinkle with nutritional yeast as soon as the egg bites come out of the oven; allow to cool slightly before serving.

Lunch

14. Sweet Potato & Collard Hash

Servings|4   Prep. Time|25 minutes   Cook Time|35-40 minutes
Nutritional Content (per serving):
Cal|166   Fat|10 g   Protein|30g   Carbs|4g

Ingredients:

1 bunch collards, stemmed & roughly chopped

1 cup red onion, finely diced

1 teaspoon salt (kosher)

1/2 cup chicken stock

1/2 teaspoon black pepper (fresh ground)

1/2 teaspoon paprika (smoked sweet)

2 sweet potatoes (medium), peeled & small diced

2 tablespoons olive oil

Directions:

1. Set the IP to SAUTE. Add the olive oil. When hot, add the onion and garlic; cook for 4 minutes or till almost translucent.
2. Add the potatoes; cook for 5 minutes or till golden. Add the collards; cook for 5 minutes or till wilted. Add the pepper, salt, and paprika; cook for 1 minute.
3. Add the broth. Lock the lid and close the pressure valve.
4. Set to MANUAL HIGH for 6 minutes. When the timer beeps, QPR and open the lid. Set the IP to SAUTE.
5. Cook for 3 minutes to reduce the cooking liquid and re-crisp the outside of the potatoes.

15. Cajun Greens

Servings|4   Prep. Time|**15 minutes**   Cook Time|**20 minutes**
Nutritional Content (per serving): Cal|**257**   Fat|**11.7g**   Protein|**22.6g**
Carbs|**15.4g**

Ingredients:

1 onion, chopped
1 pound ham (uncured), fully cooked &
chopped into large chunks
1 tablespoon bacon grease
1 turnip, chopped
1/2 cup poultry broth (use bone broth if
available)

1/8 teaspoon salt
2 teaspoons (around 2 cloves) garlic,
crushed
6 cups preferred raw greens (mustard,
kale, collard, turnip, spinach, etc.)

Directions:

1. Put everything in your IP. Lock the lid and close the pressure valve. Set to
   MANUAL HIGH pressure for 20 minutes. When the timer beeps, press CANCEL,
   NPR for 10 minutes, then QPR and open the lid. Stir the ingredients to mix them;
   serve.

16. Turnip Greens & Bacon

Servings|4   Prep. Time|15 minutes   Cook Time|30 minutes
Nutritional Content (per serving):
Cal|192   Fat|10 g   Protein|14g   Carbs|11g

Ingredients:

3-4 slices bacon, chopped into small
pieces
2 cups chicken broth
1/2 up to 1 cup ham (smoked)
necks/hocks

1/2 cup onion, diced
1 pound turnip greens (bagged)
Pepper & salt, to taste
Splash olive oil (extra-virgin)

Directions:

1. Set the IP to SAUTÉ. Add a splash of olive oil. Add the onion, bacon, and ham;
   sprinkle with pepper and salt. Sauté till the meat is cooked and the fat is
   rendered.
2. Add the broth and then the greens. Lock the lid and close the pressure valve. Set
   to HIGH pressure for 30 minutes. When the timer beeps, QPR and open the lid.
   Serve warm.

17. *Pan-Smoked Spiced Chicken Breasts with Fruit Salsa*

Servings|3   Prep. Time|15 minutes   Cook Time|20 minutes
Nutritional Content (per serving):
Cal|200   Fat|6 g   Protein|29g   Carbs|7g

Ingredients:

Paprika (1/2 tbsp)

Ground cumin (½ tsp)

Ground coriander (½ tsp)

Dried thyme (1/4 tsp)

Pepper (1/4 tsp)

Chicken breasts (3, boneless and skinless, 5 oz each)

Extra Virgin Olive Oil (as needed)

Wheatberries (9.75 oz, with Pecans and Poblanos)

Fruit Salsa (6 oz)

Salt (½ tsp)

Cilantro sprigs (as needed, for garnish, optional)

Directions:

1. Combine the cumin, paprika, thyme, salt, pepper, and coriander. Coat the breast with the spice mixture. Brush with oil lightly. Allow marinating, refrigerated, 3-4 hours.
2. Set up a smoke-roasting system. Heat the pan of sawdust or wood chips on the stovetop until smoke appears. Place the chicken on a rack and cover it.
3. Turn the heat to medium. Smoke roast 10 minutes. Transfer the pan to an oven preheated to 400 F and roast for another 10 minutes.
4. Serve wheatberries with a chicken breast on top with salsa. Top with cilantro for garnish.

18. *Buttery Lemon Chicken*

Servings|6   Prep. Time|10 minutes   Cook Time|40 minutes
Nutritional Content (per serving):
Cal|369   Fat|15 g   Protein|55g   Carbs|2g

Ingredients:

Chicken thighs (2 lbs.)

Fat free butter (2 tbsp.)

Onion (1, diced)

Chicken broth (2¼ cups, organic)

Garlic (4 cloves, minced)

Salt (1 tsp.)

Paprika (½ tsp.)

Pepper (½ tsp.)

Parsley (1 tsp., dried)

Lemon juice (1/2 cup)

Arrowroot flour (4 tsp.)

Directions:

1. Add a deep pot on medium heat, and allow to heat up. Add your fat free butter in and allow to melt.
2. Add garlic, onion, parsley, pepper, and paprika then cook until they become soft. Add your chicken pieces and allow to brown on all sides (about 3 minutes per side).
3. Season your pot with salt, then add your lemon juice, and chicken broth. Cover your lid, and allow to cook for at least 30 minutes or until chicken is fully cooked.
4. Carefully remove chicken, and set aside while you work on your sauce.
5. In a separate bowl, combine your arrowroot flour, and ¼ cup of your sauce, then stir to combine until no lumps remain.
6. In the same pot that you removed your chicken from, allow the remaining juices to come to a boil, add your arrowroot mixture and cook, while stirring, until the sauce thickens. Serve chicken covered in sauce. Enjoy.

19. *Herbed-Saffron Cauliflower Rice*

Servings|4   Prep. Time|15 minutes   Cook Time|20-25 minutes
Nutritional Content (per serving):
Cal|188   Fat|9 g   Protein|23g   Carbs|5g

Ingredients:

1 cup water, for the IP

1 head cauliflower (medium), cut into florets

1 tablespoon ghee

1 teaspoon lemon juice

1 teaspoon sea salt

1/2 teaspoon lemon zest

1/2 teaspoon saffron threads

2 cloves garlic, minced

2 tablespoons cilantro, chopped

2 tablespoons mint, chopped

Few grinds black peppers (fresh ground)

Directions:

1. Put the IP steamer basket and pour the water into the inner pot. Put the cauliflower in the basket.
2. Set to STEAM for 2 minutes. When the timer beeps, QPR and open the lid. Transfer the cauliflower to a mixing bowl. Remove the trivet and discard the water from the pot.
3. Set the IP to SAUTE. Add the ghee. When heated, add the cauliflower. With a potato masher, mash the cauliflower till the texture is rice-like.
4. Add the saffron and garlic; stir to mix. Transfer to a serving bowl. Toss with the rest of the ingredients. Serve warm.

20. *Tasty Shredded Chicken*

Servings|6   Prep. Time|37 minutes   Cook Time|15 minutes
Nutritional Content (per serving):
Cal|341   Fat|14 g   Protein|4g   Carbs|8g

Ingredients:

2 lbs. chicken breasts, skinless and boneless

1/2 cup salsa

1 tbsp olive oil

1/2 tsp oregano

1/2 tsp paprika

1 tsp garlic

1 tsp cumin

1 tbsp chili powder

14 oz can tomato, diced

7 oz can green chilies

1/2 tsp pepper

1/2 tsp salt

Directions:

1. Set a skillet with olive oil on medium heat and allow to get hot.
2. Add in your chicken breast and cook for 10 minutes, flipping at the half way point.
3. Add in your remaining ingredients, cover and cook for another 5 minutes.
4. Shred the chicken using a fork and serve with your salsa.

21. *Turkey Drumsticks*

Servings|6   Prep. Time|5 minutes   Cook Time|40 minutes
Nutritional Content (per serving):
Cal|209   Fat|6 g   Protein|35g   Carbs|3g

Ingredients:

1 tablespoon salt (kosher)   1/2 teaspoon garlic powder
1 teaspoon black pepper (fresh ground)   2 packed tight teaspoons stevia
1/2 cup coconut aminos or tamari   6 turkey drumsticks
1/2 cup water, for the IP

Directions:

1. In a bowl (small), mix the salt, stevia, pepper, and garlic powder, breaking any clumps. Season the turkey with the seasoning mixture. Pour the water and coconut aminos in the IP. Add the seasoned turkey. Lock the lid and close the pressure valve. Set to MANUAL HIGH pressure for 25 minutes.
2. When the timer beeps, press CANCEL, NPR for 15 minutes, then QPR and open the lid. Transfer the turkey to a serving dish very carefully – they will be fall-off-the-bone tender. Serve the cooking liquid as a sauce to pass at the table. If preferred, de-fat the cooking liquid before serving.

NOTES: If you prefer crisp turkey skin, brush the cooked drumsticks with some of the cooking liquid; broil till brown. The cooking liquid is also great with baked sweet potatoes.

22. *Simple Mexican Taco Wings*

Servings|6   Prep. Time|15 minutes   Cook Time|45 minutes
Nutritional Content (per serving):
Cal|212   Fat|8 g   Protein|23g   Carbs|4g

Ingredients:

1 1/3 lbs. chicken wings   1 1/2 tsp smoked salt
¼ cup taco seasoning

Directions:

1. Set your oven to preheat to 400 degrees F. Place chicken wings into the bowl and sprinkle with taco seasoning and salt. Rub seasoning over the wings.
2. Place chicken wings on a lined baking tray and set to bake for 45 minutes or until fully cooked.
3. Serve and enjoy.

Serves: 6   **Prep Time: 10 mins.**   **Cooking Time: 25 mins.**
Calories: 212   **Protein: 23.2g**   **Carbs: 4g**   **Fat: 7.5g**

23. *Chicken Fricassee*

Servings|6   Prep. Time|15 minutes   Cook Time|45 minutes
Nutritional Content (per serving):
Cal|335   Fat|10 g   Protein|30g   Carbs|33g

Ingredients:

6 large bone-in, skinless chicken thighs (2½ pounds total)
½ tsp salt
½ tsp ground black pepper
2 Tbsp fat free butter
2 leeks, white and pale green parts only, halved lengthwise, sliced, and rinsed well
3 cloves garlic, crushed with garlic press
1 tsp herbes de Provence

8 oz white mushrooms, sliced
¼ cup light sour cream
1½ pounds medium red potatoes halved
3 cup chicken broth, store-bought or homemade
1½ cups frozen peas
1 Tbsp all-purpose flour
parsley, chopped for garnish

Directions:

1. Season chicken with ½ tsp salt and ¼ tsp pepper. In a sauté pan over medium heat, melt 1 Tbsp fat free butter.
2. Add chicken to pot in batches; cook 5 minutes per side, or until browned. Transfer chicken to plate. To pot, add leeks and garlic; cook 2 minutes, stirring.
3. Return chicken to pot. Sprinkle with herbes de Provence. Top with mushrooms and potatoes; add broth. Cover with lid.
4. Set to cook for 35 minutes or until chicken is fully cooked.
5. While your chicken cooks, monitor your potatoes and transfer to large bowl when cooked.
6. In a small bowl, whisk ¼ cup sour cream and flour until smooth.
7. Once the liquid in the pot returns to a boil, stir in sour cream mixture. Simmer 2 minutes, or until thickened.
8. Coarsely mash potatoes. Add remaining 1 Tbsp fat free butter, ¼ cup sour cream, ¼ tsp salt, and ¼ tsp pepper to potatoes; mash. Serve chicken over potatoes and sprinkle with parsley.

24. *Chicken Fajitas*

Servings|6   Prep. Time|22 minutes   Cook Time|36 minutes
Nutritional Content (per serving):
Cal|326   Fat|11 g   Protein|45g   Carbs|9g

Ingredients:

2 lbs. chicken tenders, boneless

1 onion, diced

3 bell peppers, sliced

1 package taco seasoning

21 oz can tomato with green chilies, diced

Directions:

1. Add all ingredients into a pot on medium heat and stir well. Cover then allow to cook for 36 minutes or until fully cooked.
2. Serve in tortillas and enjoy.

25. *Baked Halibut Parmesan*

Servings|4   Prep. Time|10 minutes   Cook Time|15 minutes
Nutritional Content (per serving):
Cal|185   Fat|4 g   Protein|33g   Carbs|2g

Ingredients

4 halibut steaks (1½ lb.)

salt, pepper and dried basil, to taste

2 cloves garlic, crushed (or 1/2 tsp garlic powder)

2–3 tbsp fat-free yogurt

4 tsp grated Low fat parmesan cheese

paprika, to garnish

Directions:

1. Set your oven to preheat to 450°F. Arrange fish in a single layer on a non-stick or sprayed baking sheet. Sprinkle lightly with seasonings.
2. Brush the top side of fish with yogurt. Sprinkle with low fat cheese and paprika. Bake uncovered for 10 to 12 minutes, until golden. Serve immediately.

26. *Easy Pesto Fish Fillets*

Servings|4   Prep. Time|10 minutes   Cook Time|15 minutes
Nutritional Content (per serving):
Cal|157   Fat|3 g   Protein|30g   Carbs|1g

Ingredients

4 sole or whitefish fillets (1-1/2 lb/750 g)

salt and pepper, to taste

4 tsp Best-O Pesto

2 tbsp grated low-fat mozzarella or Low fat parmesan cheese

Directions

1. Set your oven to preheat to 425°F. Line a baking sheet with aluminum foil. Spray lightly with non-stick spray. Arrange fish fillets in a single layer and sprinkle lightly with salt and pepper.
2. Spread pesto evenly over fish fillets. Top with grated cheese. Bake on top rack of oven at 425°F about 10 to 12 minutes, or until low fat cheese is melted and golden. Fish should flake when lightly pressed. Serve immediately.

27. *Crispy Cheesy Baked Chicken Breasts*

Servings|4   Prep. Time|10 minutes   Cook Time|20 minutes
Nutritional Content (per serving):
Cal|239   Fat|5 g   Protein|38g   Carbs|16g

Ingredients

Chicken Cutlets (1lb, skinless, boneless)

Egg (1, whisked)

Breadcrumbs (1/4 cup, panko)

Garlic powder (1 tsp.)

Italian seasoning (1 tsp.)

Green beans (3 cups)

Olive oil (2 tsp.)

Marinara sauce (1/2 cup)

Low fat mozzarella cheese (1/2 cup, shredded)

Basil (1/4 cup, chopped)

Directions

1. Set your oven to preheat to 425 degrees F then preparing a baking sheet by lightly greasing with cooking spray. Add your Italian seasoning, garlic powder, salt, pepper, and breadcrumbs to a medium bowl.
2. Dredge your chicken into your egg then roll into your breadcrumb mixture. Carefully place the chicken onto the baking sheet then lightly drizzle with olive oil.
3. Add your green beans to a large bowl, drizzle with olive oil and season to taste. Toss to evenly coat. Add evenly around chicken pieces on the baking sheet.
4. Allow to cook until chicken has been fully cooked through (about 15 minutes).
5. When cooked, use your sauce and low fat cheese to top your chicken pieces then return to the oven until your low fat cheese is melted (about another 2 minutes). Serve, and enjoy.

28. *Chicken Souvlaki Kebobs*

Servings|4   Prep. Time|5 minutes   Cook Time|15 minutes
Nutritional Content (per serving):
Cal|189   Fat|9 g   Protein|20g   Carbs|7g

Ingredients

12 oz (3/4 lb.) boneless skinless chicken
1 lemon
2 garlic cloves
1/2 small white onion
1/2 yellow bell pepper
1/2 cup grape tomato

1 teaspoon dried oregano
3/4 teaspoon Celtic sea salt
2 tablespoons coconut oil
8 skewers

Directions

1. Soak wooden skewers in water for 10 minutes, if using. Juice lemon into medium mixing bowl. Peel and mince garlic.
2. Remove stem, seeds and veins from bell pepper. Peel onion. Roughly chop pepper and onion.
3. Add to bowl with tomatoes, 1 tablespoon coconut oil, oregano and salt. Pierce chicken multiple times with fork, then cut into one-inch chunks.
4. Add to bowl and mix to combine. Let set aside in refrigerator for 10 minutes. Heat small skillet or griddle over medium-high heat and add 1 tablespoon coconut oil.
5. Drain marinated chicken and veggies, then carefully add to skewer, alternating meat and veggies. Add chicken and veggie skewer to hot oiled skillet or griddle.
6. Grill for about 1 - 2 minutes then turn 1/4 the way around. Continue cooking and turning until chicken is golden brown and cooked through. Remove from heat and serve immediately.

29. *Lemon Garlic Chicken*

Servings|4   Prep. Time|15 minutes   Cook Time|30 minutes
Nutritional Content (per serving):
Cal|460   Fat|9 g   Protein|67g   Carbs|5g

Ingredients:

1 Tbsp coconut oil

1 onion, diced

2 lb chicken breasts

5 cloves garlic, minced

1 tsp salt

1 tsp dried parsley

½ cup chicken broth

¼ cup white cooking wine

¼ tsp paprika

1 Tbsp lemon juice

3 tsp arrowroot flour

Directions:

1. Set your Instant Pot to Sauté. Add the avocado oil. Add onions and cook for 5 minutes. Add the rest of the ingredients, except for the flour. Cover the pot. Choose the poultry setting.
2. Cook for 25 minutes. Release the pressure naturally. Take ¼ cup of the cooking liquid from the pot. Add the arrowroot flour to this liquid. Pour it back into the pot. Stir well. Serve while warm.

30. *Spicy Cilantro Lime Chicken*

Servings|4   Prep. Time|10 minutes   Cook Time|10 minutes
Nutritional Content (per serving):
Cal|247   Fat|10 g   Protein|36g   Carbs|5g

Ingredients

1-pound boneless, skinless chicken breasts

Juice from 2 limes, divided

5 garlic cloves

½ tablespoon cumin

1 teaspoon chili powder

½ cup non-fat Greek yogurt

1 jalapeño (seeds and stems removed)

1 cup freshly chopped cilantro

⅛ teaspoon salt

⅛ teaspoon black pepper

Directions

1. Place the chicken in a large Ziploc bag. Add ½ of lime juice, 3 garlic cloves, cumin, and chili powder. With bag sealed, massage chicken with marinade and refrigerate for at least one hour (or up to 8 hours in advance).
2. Preheat grill to medium. Place chicken on grill (discard marinade) and cook until juices run clear or reaches an internal temperature of 165°F.
3. Let the chicken rest for 10 minutes. To make the sauce, in a small bowl blend the remaining lime juice, garlic, yogurt, jalapeño, cilantro, salt, and pepper until smooth. Set aside. Top chicken with one tablespoon of green cilantro sauce and serve.

31. *Slow Cooker Fresh Turkey Chili*

Servings|12   Prep. Time|20 minutes   Cook Time|5 hours
Nutritional Content (per serving):
Cal|134   Fat|5 g   Protein|13g   Carbs|10g

Ingredients

1 pound of lean ground turkey
1 large green and 1 large red bell pepper, both seeded and diced
2 tbsp. chili powder
1 can crushed tomatoes
1 chopped sweet onion

2 T tomato paste
1 T minced fresh garlic
2 t cumin
1 can kidney beans, drained and rinsed
½ cup diced green chilies
Black pepper for taste

Directions

1. Cook your turkey with the garlic in a skillet, using it to pull apart the meat until it is browned. Take off any fat and then add in the bell peppers until they are soft, usually about 5 minutes.
2. Add in the chili powder and the cumin. Put the ingredients into a slow cooker and then let it sit for about 4-5 hours. You can season to taste with black pepper.

32. *Stir Fried Chicken*

Servings|6   Prep. Time|12 minutes   Cook Time|5 minutes
Nutritional Content (per serving):
Cal|214   Fat|9 g   Protein|24g   Carbs|10g

Ingredients:

3 chicken breasts, cubed
1 1/2 tbsp sesame seeds
1/2 cup coconut aminos
1 tsp garlic, minced
2 green onion, sliced
3 cups asparagus, cut into pieces

3 bell peppers, diced
1 onion, diced
1 tbsp sesame oil
Pepper
Salt

Directions:

1. Add sesame oil into the instant pot and select sauté. Add chicken into the pot and sauté until chicken almost done. Add in the rest if your remaining ingredients and stir well.
2. Seal pot with lid and select steam for 2 minutes. Release pressure using quick release then open the lid. Stir and serve.

33. *Spinach Turkey Burgers*

Servings|4   Prep. Time|15 minutes   Cook Time|20 minutes
Nutritional Content (per serving):
Cal|200   Fat|11 g   Protein|24g   Carbs|2g

Ingredients:

1-pound ground turkey (93 to 95% lean)
1 garlic clove, minced
¾ cup frozen chopped spinach, thawed
Zest of 1 lemon
1 egg

¼ teaspoon salt
¼ teaspoon black pepper
4 small whole wheat rolls
4 lettuce leaves (garnish)
4 tomato slices (garnish)
4 red onion slices (garnish)

Directions:

1. In a large bowl, combine turkey, garlic, spinach, lemon zest, egg, salt, and pepper. Mix well with hands. Form mixture into 4 patties. Heat grill pan or grill to medium-high heat.
2. Cook for 5 to 7 minutes on each side or until cooked throughout or reaches an internal temperature of 165°F. Place cooked patties between rolls. Top with lettuce, tomato, onion and your favorite condiment.
3. Cook until low fat cheese is melted and bread is toasted, about 2 to 3 minutes on each side.

34. *Thai Green Curry Chicken*

Servings|1   Prep. Time|15 minutes   Cook Time|4 hours 30 minutes
Nutritional Content (per serving):
Cal|298   Fat|11 g   Protein|36g   Carbs|6g

Ingredients

1 ½ Cans Light Coconut Milk
3 Tbsp. Green Curry Paste
4 Garlic Cloves
3 Tbsp. Stevia
2 ½ lbs. Chicken Breast, Cut into Chunks

1 Bag Stir Fry Vegetables
1 Red Onions
1 Can Mini Corn
2 Tbsp. Cornstarch

Directions

1. Whisk together the coconut milk, curry paste, garlic cloves, and stevia. Add the chicken, baby corn, onion, and vegetables. Then cook for four hours on low.
2. After the cooking is finished, whisk together the cornstarch, and add 2 tablespoons of water. Cook everything for another thirty minutes or when the curry is thickened.

35. *Coriander Crusted Salmon & Asparagus Salad*

Servings|4   Prep. Time|15 minutes   Cook Time|3 minutes
Nutritional Content (per serving):
Cal|288   Fat|10 g   Protein|31g   Carbs|4g

Ingredients:

1 tsp lemon zest

½ tsp red pepper, crushed

1 Tbsp coriander seeds

¾ tsp fine sea salt, divided

1 lb wild salmon, sliced into 4 portions

2 cups water

1 lb asparagus, trimmed

2 Tbsp olive oil

1 Tbsp lemon juice

1 Tbsp fresh tarragon, chopped

1 Tbsp fresh mint, chopped

¼ tsp ground pepper

Directions:

1. Put the lemon zest, red pepper, coriander seeds and ½ tsp salt in a spice grinder. Pulse until finely ground. Cover the salmon with spice mixture. Pour the water into Instant Pot.
2. Place a steamer inside. Place the salmon and asparagus onto the steamer. Close the pot. Set it to Manual. Cook on high for 3 minutes. Release the pressure quickly.
3. In a bowl, mix the olive oil, lemon juice, tarragon, mint, and pepper. Toss the asparagus in this dressing. Serve the salmon with the asparagus salad.

36. *Pizza Fish Fillets*

Servings|4   Prep. Time|10 minutes   Cook Time|15 minutes
Nutritional Content (per serving):
Cal|169   Fat|3 g   Protein|30g   Carbs|3g

Ingredients

6 sole fillets

salt and pepper, to taste

1/2 cup pizza or tomato sauce

2 tbsp chopped mushrooms

3 tbsp minced green pepper or zucchini

1/2 cup grated low-fat low fat mozzarella cheese

Directions

1. Set your oven to preheat to 425°F. Spray a foil-lined baking sheet with non-stick spray. Arrange fish in a single layer. Sprinkle lightly with salt and pepper.

2. Spread sauce evenly over fish. Sprinkle with vegetables; top with cheese. Bake uncovered at 425°F for 10 to 12 minutes, or until golden. Fish should flake easily when tested with a fork. Serve immediately.

37. *Chicken Cacciatore*

Servings|4   Prep. Time|10 minutes   Cook Time|25 minutes
Nutritional Content (per serving):
Cal|295   Fat|9 g   Protein|31g   Carbs|21g

Ingredients:

1 8-oz package sliced cremini mushrooms
1 Tbsp olive oil
1 medium onion, thinly sliced
3 cloves garlic, thinly sliced
2 Tbsp all-purpose flour
1 28-oz can diced tomatoes
1¼ tsp dried oregano
¼ tsp salt

¼ tsp crushed red pepper flakes
4 bone-in, skinless chicken thighs (about 8 oz each)
bell pepper, 1 medium, thinly sliced
3 Tbsp chopped fresh basil or parsley
1 tsp balsamic vinegar
Freshly grated Low fat parmesan cheese, for serving

Directions:

1. Set you IP on the Sauté more and set on High. Cook mushrooms in oil, uncovered, for 4 minutes. Stir in onion and garlic; cook 4 minutes, or until onions soften.
2. Sprinkle in flour and stir. Then add tomatoes, oregano, salt, and pepper flakes. Stir and scrape up any browned bits on pan bottom. Add chicken thighs, pressing into the sauce. Close your IP.
3. Set on Pressure Cook or Manual mode then set on High for 9 minutes. When done, open the vent to release pressure. Transfer chicken to plate.
4. Stir and scrape any bits off the bottom of the pan if needed. Choose Sauté function and adjust heat to More.
5. Stir in bell pepper and cook 4 minutes, or until peppers are just tender. Stir in basil and balsamic vinegar. Serve with grated Parmesan.

38. *BBQ Chicken Drumsticks*

Servings|6   Prep. Time|5 minutes   Cook Time|25 minutes
Nutritional Content (per serving):
Cal|179   Fat|5 g   Protein|26g   Carbs|5g

Ingredients:
To Clean Chicken:
Water (3 cups)
Vinegar (1/2 cup, white distilled)
BBQ Chicken Drumsticks:
2 lbs. of chicken drumsticks
2 tablespoons sweet paprika
3 teaspoons black pepper

1 tablespoon salt
1 teaspoon cayenne pepper
2 teaspoons garlic powder
1 teaspoon ginger powder
½ teaspoon cinnamon powder
2 teaspoons dry mustard
2 tablespoons cumin powder

Directions:
1. Combine your water and vinegar in a large bowl, and stir to combine. Add your chicken straight from the pack and let stand for 3 minutes. Drain chicken and rinse under cold water. Set aside.
2. Add 1 cup of water to Instant Pot. Set trivet inside the pot. Arrange chicken drumsticks on a trivet. Cover pot with lid and set it on "POULTRY" mode, cook for 20 minutes.
3. Meanwhile, set your oven to preheat to Broil. Place parchment paper on the baking tray. When the timer goes off, press 'cancel,' and allow to cool down naturally for about 20 minutes before attempting to open.
4. Remove drumsticks from the pot and rub them with BBQ spices and place them on a baking tray. Set to broil for 2 minutes per side or till nicely browned. Serve and enjoy.

39. *Tuna Casserole*

Servings|4   Prep. Time|10 minutes   Cook Time|7 minutes
Nutritional Content (per serving):
Cal|139   Fat|1 g   Protein|20g   Carbs|13g

Ingredients:

1 package of egg noodles
2 cups of frozen green peas
2 cans of mushroom soup
2 cans of tuna drained

1 onion chopped
10 slices of processed low fat cheese
black pepper to taste

Directions:

1. Set a decent sized pot on with water and allow to boil. Once boiling, add in peas and noodles. Allow to cook until the noodles are fork tender, then drain.
2. Return your peas and noodles to the pot. Mix pepper, low fat cheese, onions, tuna and soup. Cook, while stirring, until your low fat cheese melts.

40. *Turkey Breasts with Wilted Spinach*

Servings|1   Prep. Time|15 minutes   Cook Time|30 minutes
Nutritional Content (per serving):
Cal|216   Fat|1 g   Protein|42g   Carbs|6g

Ingredients:

Turkey breast (125 grams, cleaned and dried)

Spinach (1 cup, cooked)
Salt, and pepper (1 tsp. each)

Directions:

1. Set your oven to preheat to 400 degrees F and prepare a baking sheet by lining it with aluminum foil. Lay your turkey breast on the baking sheet, and season with salt, and pepper.
2. Set to bake until turkey breast has been fully cooked (about 30 minutes). Remove from oven and let stand at room temperature for about 5 minutes before servings. Serve alongside reheated spinach.

Dinner

41. Chicken Shawarma

Servings|6   Prep. Time|1 hour   Cook Time|4 minutes
Nutritional Content (per serving):
Cal|216   Fat|7g   Protein|33g   Carbs|2g

Ingredients:

1 teaspoon garlic powder
1 teaspoon onion powder
1/2 teaspoon pepper
1/2 teaspoon salt
1/4 teaspoon cinnamon
1/4 teaspoon turmeric

2 pounds chicken breasts/thighs
(skinless & boneless)
2 tablespoons lemon juice
2 tablespoons olive oil
2 teaspoons cumin
2 teaspoons paprika

Directions:

1   Mix the chicken with the rest of the ingredients. Refrigerate and marinate for at least 1 hour or overnight. Add the chicken and the marinade in your IP. Lock the lid and close the pressure valve. Set to MANUAL for 8 minutes.

2   When the timer beeps, press CANCEL, NPR completely, then QPR and open the lid. Shred the chicken meat. Serve as desired.

42. Salmon & Broccoli

Servings|1   Prep. Time|1 minutes   Cook Time|2 minutes
Nutritional Content (per serving):
Cal|145   Fat|5.7g   Protein|17.7g   Carbs|6.5g

Ingredients:

72 grams salmon fillet
70 grams broccoli, chopped

Pepper & salt
160 ml water

Directions:

1.   Put the IP steamer basket and pour the water into the inner pot. Season the salmon and broccoli with pepper and salt.

2.   Put the fish the veggie in the basket. Lock the lid and close the pressure valve. Set to STEAM for 2 minutes.

3.   When the timer beeps, press CANCEL, NPR completely, then QPR and open the lid.

43. *Chicken Paillard with Grilled Vegetables*

Servings|4   Prep. Time|12 minutes   Cook Time|15 - 20 minutes
Nutritional Content (per serving):
Cal|250   Fat|11 g   Protein|34g   Carbs|1g

Ingredients:

Chicken breast (4 boneless, skinless about 6 oz each)

Garlic cloves (1, chopped)

Fresh rosemary (1/3 tbsp, chopped)

Salt (1/4 tsp)

Pepper (1/8 tsp)

Lemon juice (1 fl oz)

Olive oil (1 fl oz)

Grilled vegetable medley (as desired)

Fresh rosemary (4 sprigs)

Directions:

1. Place each chicken breast between sheets of plastic film. With a meat mallet, carefully pound to a uniform thickness of about ¼ in.
2. Combine the garlic, rosemary, salt, and pepper then use to season both sides of your chicken. Sprinkle with lemon juice then olive oil and allow to marinate for at least 2 hours in the refrigerator.
3. Set your grill to preheat on high. Place the chicken breasts and veggies on the grill or under your broiler, skin side (that is, the side that had the skin on) down, and grill until about one-fourth has done. Rotate on the grill to mark. Continue to cook until about half has done. Turnover and continue to grill until just cooked through.
4. Plate and serve. Garnish with a sprig of rosemary.

44. Baked Fish with Tomatoes and Mushrooms

Servings|4   Prep. Time|12 minutes   Cook Time|25 minutes
Nutritional Content (per serving):
Cal|350   Fat|9 g   Protein|55 g   Carbs|6g

Ingredients:

Fish (4, whole and small, 12 oz each)

Salt (to taste)

Pepper (to taste)

Dried thyme (pinch)

Parsley (4 sprigs)

Olive oil (as needed)

Onion (4 oz, small dice)

Shallots (1 oz, minced)

Mushrooms (8 oz, chopped)

Tomato concasse (6.4 oz)

Dry white wine (3.2 fl oz)

Directions:

1. Scale and clean the fish but leaves the heads on. Season the fish inside and out with salt and pepper and put a small pinch of thyme and a sprig of parsley in the cavity of each.
2. Use as many baking pans to hold the fish in a single layer. Oil the pans with a little olive oil.
3. Sauté the onions and shallots in a little olive oil about 1 minute. Add the mushrooms and sauté lightly.
4. Put the sautéed vegetables and the tomatoes in the bottoms of the baking pans.
5. Put the fish in the pans. Oil the tops lightly. Pour in the wine.
6. Bake at 400F until the fish is done. The time will vary but will average 15-20 minutes. Base often with the liquid in the pan.
7. Remove the fish and keep them warm until they are plated.
8. Remove the vegetables from the pans with a slotted spoon and check for seasonings. Serve a spoonful of the vegetables with the fish, placing it under or alongside each fish.
9. Strain, degrease, and reduce the cooking liquid slightly. Just before serving, moisten each portion with 1-2 tbsp of the liquid.

45. _Steamed Shrimp & Asparagus_

Servings|2-4   Prep. Time|20 minutes   Cook Time|2 minutes
Nutritional Content (per serving):
Cal|329   Fat|6.4g   Protein|56.1g   Carbs|11.1g

Ingredients:

1 bunch (around 6 ounces) asparagus

1 pound shrimp (fresh/frozen), peeled & deveined

1 teaspoon olive oil

1/2 tablespoon Cajun seasoning, lemon juice w/ pepper & salt, or preferred seasoning

Directions:

1. Put the IP trivet and pour 1 cup water in the inner pot. Arrange the asparagus in a single layer on the trivet. Put the shrimps on top of them.
2. Drizzle the shrimps with the oil and sprinkle with the seasoning.
3. Lock the lid and close the pressure valve. Set to STEAM LOW pressure for 2 minutes frozen or for 1 minute for fresh shrimp.
4. When the timer beeps, QPR and open the lid. Serve.

46. _Creamy Garlic Pepper Chicken_

Servings|3   Prep. Time|15 minutes   Cook Time|8 minutes
Nutritional Content (per serving):
Cal|305   Fat|12 g   Protein|28g   Carbs|13g

Ingredients:

8 oz chicken breasts, skinless and boneless, cut into pieces

1/2 cup sour cream

2 cups chicken broth

2 tbsp garlic powder

1 medium onion, sliced

1 red pepper, sliced

1 green pepper, sliced

Directions:

1. Transfer ingredients to your IP and stir well. Cover then allow to cook on manual high pressure for 8 minutes.
2. Do a natural pressure release before opening the lid. Serve and enjoy.

47. Chicken 2-Ways

Servings|4   Prep. Time|5 minutes   Cook Time|15 minutes
Nutritional Content (per serving):
Cal|180   Fat|0g   Protein|33.4g   Carbs|2g

Ingredients:

1 pound frozen chicken breasts, (skinless & boneless)

Preferred flavorful cooking liquid, see options below

Flavorful cooking liquid options:

Lemon Garlic Herb:

1/2 cup water

1/2 of a lemon juice

2 cloves garlic, minced

1/2 teaspoon basil (dried)

Pepper & salt

Thai Curry:

1 cup coconut milk (canned)

1-2 tablespoon preferred Thai curry paste

Directions:

1. In a bowl (small) or measuring cup, mix your choice of flavorful cooking liquid. Put the chicken in the IP. Add the liquid, pouring it over the chicken. Lock the lid and close the pressure valve.
2. Set to POULTRY for 15 minutes for standard 4-8 ounces pieces or for 30 minutes for extra-large ones, around 1 pound each piece. When the timer beeps, QPR and open the lid.
3. Transfer the chicken to a large plate or cutting board. Shred into bite-sized pieces using 2 forks. While shredding the meat, set the IP to SAUTÉ and cook the sauce to reduce and thicken if too thin.
4. Once thick to preference, return the shredded chicken to the pot; toss to coat with the sauce.

48. 30-Minute Fall-Off-The-Bone Chicken

Servings|10   Prep. Time|10 minutes   Cook Time|35 minutes
Nutritional Content (per serving):
Cal|297   Fat|7.2g   Protein|53.5g   Carbs|1.1g

Ingredients:

1 1/2 cups bone broth (chicken)

1 tablespoon coconut oil (virgin)

1 teaspoon paprika

1 teaspoon thyme (dried)

1 whole (around 4 pounds) chicken

1/2 teaspoon sea salt

1/4 teaspoon black pepper (fresh ground)

2 tablespoons lemon juice (fresh squeezed)

6 cloves garlic, peeled

Directions:

1. In a bowl (small), mix the thyme, paprika, salt, and pepper. Rub the outside of your chicken with the spice mixture. Set the IP to SAUTÉ.
2. Add the oil. When hot and shimmering, add the chicken breast with the breast side down.
3. Cook for 6 up to 7 minutes. Rotate the chicken. Add the broth, lemon juice, and garlic cloves.
4. Lock the lid and close the pressure valve. Set to MANUAL HIGH pressure for 25 minutes. When the timer beeps, press CANCEL, NPR completely, then QPR and open the lid.
5. Transfer the chicken to a serving platter; let stand for 5 minutes. Carve and serve.

49. *Chicken Legs W/ Lemon & Garlic*

Servings|4   Prep. Time|5 minutes   Cook Time|25 minutes
Nutritional Content (per serving):
Cal|149   Fat|5g   Protein|22.2g   Carbs|3g

Ingredients:

1 cup water

1 frozen package chicken legs

1 lemon, quartered

1 teaspoon Italian herbs seasoning

1 teaspoon salt

1/4 teaspoon pepper

8 garlic cloves, peeled

Directions:

1. Put the water and garlic in your IP. Add the chicken; season with the pepper, salt, and seasoning. Put the lemon on top of the meat.
2. Lock the lid and close the pressure valve. Set to MANUAL for 25 minutes. When the timer beeps, QPR and open the lid. Serve.

50. *Duck Confit*

Servings|4   Prep. Time|24 hours   Cook Time|2 hours
Nutritional Content (per serving):
Cal|205   Fat|10.5g   Protein|24.9g   Carbs|1.24g

Ingredients:

1 tablespoon salt (kosher)
2 bay leaves, torn into halves
4 pieces duck legs (thighs & drumsticks)
1/4 teaspoon black peppercorns (fresh ground), lightly crushed

4 garlic cloves, smashed
1/4 teaspoon allspice berries, crushed lightly
3   sprigs thyme (fresh)

Directions:

1. Line a plate or rimmed sheet pan with some paper towels. Mix the allspice, peppercorns, bay leaves, garlic, thyme, and salt in a bowl (large).
2. Add your duck legs; toss to coat well with the spice mixture. In a single layer, put the duck in the prepared sheet pan/plate; refrigerate without cover for a minimum of 24 hours up to three (3) days.
3. Brush off the thyme sprigs and garlic off the duck; reserve them. Set the IP to SAUTE. With the skin-side down, arrange the duck legs in your pot with the flesh in contact with the pot bottom as much as possible.
4. Cook for 5 up to 10 minutes or till golden brown and the fat begins to render. Flip the duck; cook for 5 up to ten (10) minutes more. Scatter the reserved thyme and garlic over the duck.
5. Lock the lid and close the pressure valve. Set for forty (40) minutes on HIGH pressure. When the timer beeps, press CANCEL, NPR completely, then QPR and open the lid. Let the poultry cool completely.
6. Store it with covered with its own fat and cooking juices in the fridge. As the dark brown sauce cools, the duck fat will separate; save this for soups, sauces, or any dish needing concentrated poultry or meat stock.
7. When ready to serve; preheat your broiler. Remove the fat off the duck legs. Put them to a sheet pan with rim.
8. Broil for 3 up to five (5) minutes or till the skin is crisp. Or crisp the skin in a dry, hot pan/skillet.

51. Classic Chicken Shawarma

Servings|6   Prep. Time|25 minutes   Cook Time|1 hour 15 minutes
Nutritional Content (per serving):
Cal|236   Fat|9.3g   Protein|35.3g   Carbs|0.9g

Ingredients:

1 1/2 lbs. chicken breasts, skinless and boneless
1 tsp ground allspice
2½ cups chicken broth
1/8 tsp ground cinnamon
1/2 tsp turmeric

1 tsp paprika
1/2 lb. chicken thighs, skinless and boneless
1/4 tsp chili powder
1/4 tsp granulated garlic

Directions:

1. Slice chicken thighs and chicken breast into strips and place in a deep pot. In a small bowl, combine together all spices.
2. Sprinkle spices mix over the chicken strips. Mix well to coat chicken with spices. Pour broth on top of chicken.
3. Cover pot with lid and set over medium heat to cook for an hour and 15 minutes or until fully cooked.
4. Serve and enjoy.

52. Slow-Cooked Rosemary-Lemon Lamb

Servings|8-10   Prep. Time|5 minutes   Cook Time|6-8 hours
Nutritional Content (per serving):
Cal|310   Fat|12.1g   Protein|46g   Carbs|1.2g

Ingredients:

1 boneless (around 4 - 5 pounds) leg lamb
1 lemon, sliced
2 cups water

2 sprigs rosemary
2 tablespoon Dijon mustard or 4 cloves garlic, chopped
Pepper & salt

Directions:

1. Put the lemon slices and the sprigs of rosemary in the bottom of your IP. Put the lamb on top of lemon and rosemary. Generously with salt and pepper. Add the mustard or cloves on top of the lamb.
2. Add the water. Lock the lid and close the pressure valve. Set to SLOW COOK NORMAL mode for 6 up to 8 hours.
3. When the timer beeps, QPR and open the lid. Serve with mashed sweet potatoes.

53. *Flounder in Stewed Tomatoes*

Servings|4   Prep. Time|15 minutes   Cook Time|25 minutes
Nutritional Content (per serving):
Cal|257   Fat|7.2g   Protein|32.4g   Carbs|10.3g

Ingredients:

1 Tbsp olive oil

1 onion, chopped

2 cloves garlic, chopped

½ sweet red pepper, chopped

½ cup white wine

14 ½ oz canned stewed tomatoes

1 Tbsp capers

12 Kalamata olives, pitted and sliced in half

1 tbsp lemon juice

1 tsp lemon zest

½ tsp dried oregano

¼ tsp salt

1/8 tsp black pepper

4 flounder fillets

Directions:

1 Set your IP on Sauté mode. Add the oil. Cook the onions, garlic, and red peppers for 2 minutes. Add the wine, tomatoes, capers, olives, lemon juice, lemon zest, oregano, salt, and pepper. Simmer for 10 minutes.

2 Add the fish fillet. Cover the pot. Turn it to Manual. Cook on low for 10 minutes. Serve with bread or a green salad.

54. *Simple Moist Turkey Breast*

Servings|8   Prep. Time|30 minutes   Cook Time|1 hour 30 minutes
Nutritional Content (per serving):
Cal|360   Fat|5.8g   Protein|58.3g   Carbs|14g

Ingredients:

6 lbs. turkey breast

1 celery rib, cut into 1inch pieces

3 cups chicken stock

1 tsp thyme

1 onion, peeled and quartered

Pepper

Salt

Directions:

1. Pour chicken broth into a deep pot. Add celery, onion, and thyme into the chicken broth. Season turkey breast with pepper and salt.
2. Place your seasoned turkey breast into the pot.
3. Cover then allow to cook on medium heat for 1 hour and 30 minutes or until fully cooked.
4. Transfer turkey breast on serving platter. Cut turkey breast into the slices and serve.

55. *Mediterranean Tuna Steaks*

Servings|3   Prep. Time|8 minutes   Cook Time|6 minutes
Nutritional Content (per serving):
Cal|230   Fat|13g   Protein|26g   Carbs|3g

Ingredients

2 tablespoons extra virgin olive oil, divided

3 tablespoons lemon juice

1 teaspoon lemon zest

1 clove of garlic, minced

⅓ cup Italian flat leaf parsley, finely chopped

⅓ cup fresh basil, finely chopped

⅛ teaspoon salt, divided

¼ teaspoon freshly ground black pepper, divided

3 tuna steaks (4 ounces each)

Directions

1. In a small bowl, combine 1 tablespoon olive oil, lemon juice and zest, garlic, parsley, basil, and half of salt and pepper. Whisk well and set aside.
2. Brush tuna steaks on both sides with 1 tablespoon of olive oil and season with remaining salt and pepper. Heat a grill or grill pan on high heat. Add steaks.
3. Cook 3 minutes on each side or until tuna reaches an internal temperature of 145°F.
4. Place steaks on plate and top with two tablespoons of lemon and herb mixture. Serve immediately.

56. Lamb Leg

Servings|8-10   Prep. Time|5 minutes   Cook Time|35 minutes
Nutritional Content (per serving):
Cal|264   Fat|12.6g   Protein|34.6g   Carbs|1.1g

Ingredients:

1 boneless (3 to 4 pounds) lamb legs

2 cups water

2 tablespoon rosemary (fresh), chopped

2 tablespoons avocado oil, divided

4 cloves garlic, crushed

Pepper & salt

Directions:

1. Pat dry the lamb with paper towels; season with pepper and salt. Set your IP to SAUTE. Add the oil. When hot, add the lamb and cook till all the sides brown. Transfer the lamb to a plate. Rub and spread the sides and top with the garlic and rosemary.

2. Put the IP trivet and pour the water into the inner pot. Put the lamb on the trivet. Lock the lid and close the pressure valve. Set to MEAT/STEW for 30 up to 35 minutes or depending on how done you want it. Thirty (30) minutes is enough to cook a 4-pound leg to medium-rare. When the timer beeps, press CANCEL, NPR completely, then QPR and open the lid.

3. Preheat your broiler. Put the lamb in a broiling pan; broil 6-inch from the heat source for 2 minutes or till the top is brown. Transfer to a serving dish; let rest for 10 minutes before slicing.

57. *Micro-Poached Salmon Fillets*

Servings|4   Prep. Time|15 minutes   Cook Time|10 minutes
Nutritional Content (per serving):
Cal|246   Fat|11g   Protein|34g   Carbs|1g

Ingredients

Romaine or iceberg lettuce leaves

4 salmon fillets, skinned

salt and pepper, to taste

1 tbsp dill, minced

1 tbsp lemon or lime juice

additional lemon slices or dill, for garnish

Directions

1. Arrange a half of your washed lettuce leaves in the bottom of your pie plate. Add your fish on top. Ensure the thicker edges are toward the outside edge of the dish.
2. Season then sprinkle with lemon juice; add your dill on top. Top with the rest of your lettuce.
3. Set to microwave for 3 minutes on High. Rotate the dish and cook fish 3 minutes longer. Fish should be even in color.
4. Let fish stand covered for 3 to 4 minutes. If it doesn't flake when pressed lightly, microwave or another minute or two more. Discard lettuce and use dill to garnish. Delicious hot or cold.

58. Garlic Bacon and low-fat cheese Stuffed Chicken Breasts

Servings|4   Prep. Time|10 minutes   Cook Time|35 minutes
Nutritional Content (per serving):
Cal|324   Fat|12.1g   Protein|39.2g   Carbs|7.7g

Ingredients

6 oz. chicken breasts, skinless

1 egg, beaten

2 tbsp. egg whites

2 ½ pounds bread crumbs

1 ½ tbsp. low fat parmesan cheese, grated

2 tbsp. flour

1 ½ tsp. garlic powder

1 tsp Italian seasoning

4-ounce light low fat cream cheese, softened

3 slices of bacon, cooked and crumbled

1 oz. low fat mozzarella cheese, shredded

Directions

1. Preheat the oven to 3750F. Cut the chicken breasts open until it resembles a fat free butterfly. Mix together the egg and egg whites in a bowl. Set aside.
2. In another bowl, combine the bread crumbs, low fat parmesan cheese, flour, garlic powder, and Italian seasoning.
3. In another bowl, combine the low fat cream cheese, and mozzarella cheese. Place a tbsp of the low fat cheese mixture into the middle of the chicken breasts.
4. Place the flaps of meat over to close over the mixture. Secure with toothpicks. Submerge the chicken in the egg mixture and dredge into the bread crumbs mixture.
5. Place on a baking sheet. Spray with cooking spray. Bake for 35 minutes until golden brown.

59. *One Pan Lemon Garlic Chicken and Asparagus*

Servings|4   Prep. Time|5 minutes   Cook Time|20 minutes
Nutritional Content (per serving):
Cal|239   Fat|5g   Protein|38g   Carbs|10g

Ingredients

Chicken breast (1.33 lbs., skinless, boneless)
Flour (2 tbsp.)
Garlic powder (1 tsp.)
Pepper (1/2 tsp.)
Salt (1/2 tsp.)

Lemon (1, zested, juiced)
Olive oil (1 tbsp.)
Asparagus (2 cups, chopped)
Garlic (2 cloves, minced)
Chicken broth (1/2 cup, low sodium)
Vinegar (1 tbsp., white wine)

Directions

1. Add lemon zest, garlic powder, and flour to a large bowl then season to taste. Add your chicken pieces to the mixture and toss to coat.
2. Set a skillet with oil over medium heat and allow to get hot. Once hot, add your chicken and allow to cook until brown on both sides (about 3 minutes per side). Set aside.
3. Set the skillet back on medium heat, add garlic, and asparagus then cook, while stirring, for 3 minutes.
4. Add vinegar, and chicken broth then stir, ensuring that you scrape in the brown bits from the bottom of the pot.
5. Return your chicken pieces to the pot, stir, and allow to cook until fully cooked (about 10 minutes). Top with lemon juice. Serve, and enjoy!

60. *Baked Herbed Fish Fillets*

Servings|4   Prep. Time|10 minutes   Cook Time|15 minutes
Nutritional Content (per serving):
Cal|163   Fat|4.1g   Protein|29g   Carbs|1g

Ingredients

4 sole, doré or orange roughy fillets
2 tsp olive or canola oil
2 cloves garlic, minced

2 tbsp fresh orange, lemon or lime juice
salt, pepper and paprika, to taste
2 tbsp each fresh dill and basil, minced

Directions

1. Set your oven to preheat to 425°F. Arrange fish in a single layer on a non-stick or sprayed pan. Brush both sides of fish lightly with oil.
2. Sprinkle evenly with garlic, citrus juice and seasonings. Bake uncovered for 10 to 12 minutes. Fish should flake easily when tested with a fork.

61. *Creamy Salmon Paté*

Servings|12   Prep. Time|25 minutes   Cook Time|0 minutes
Nutritional Content (per serving):
Cal|55   Fat|1.6g   Protein|8g   Carbs|2g

Ingredients

4 green onions, minced
2 tbsp fresh dill, minced
1/2 lb. smooth low fat cottage cheese or
low-fat low fat cream cheese

1/4 cup non-fat yogurt or sour cream
7-1/2 oz can (213 g) salmon, drained
1 tsp lemon juice (preferably fresh)
freshly ground pepper

Directions

1. Combine all ingredients and mix until blended. (If using the processor, first mince green onions and dill, then add remaining ingredients and process just until blended.)
2. Chill before serving. Serve as a spread with low GI crackers, breads or fresh veggies, or use as a sandwich filling. If desired, garnish with finely minced red onion, thinly sliced cucumber and/or dill.

62. *Honey Mustard Chicken Drumsticks*

Servings|6   Prep. Time|30 minutes   Cook Time|1 hour
Nutritional Content (per serving):
Cal|93.3   Fat|2.9g   Protein|12.9g   Carbs|3.9g

Ingredients

3 lbs. drumsticks
4 oz. flour
1 tsp. salt
½ tsp. paprika
1 tsp. white pepper
½ tsp. chicken seasoning

½ cup soft fat free butter
½ cup honey
½ cup mustard
6 tsp. lime juice
½ tsp. salt

Directions

1. Wash and drain drumsticks. Use a clean cloth or paper towel to dry chicken. In a paper bag, combine salt, almond flour, paprika, chicken seasoning and white pepper.
2. Put chicken in bag and shake vigorously to coat properly. Melt fat free butter in a baking pan, roll pieces of chicken in melted fat free butter until all sides are coated.
3. Fix the chicken pieces, skin side down in the baking pan, packing them close to each other but not overcrowded. Bake at 400 degrees F for 30 minutes.
4. Turn chicken pieces over and pour on glaze. Bake for a further 20 minutes or when your cooked. Set aside.
5. Mix all ingredients together and pour over chicken and serve.

63. *Sheet Pan Healthy Chicken Parmesan*

Servings|4   Prep. Time|10 minutes   Cook Time|20 minutes
Nutritional Content (per serving):
Cal|239   Fat|5g   Protein|38g   Carbs|1g

Ingredients

¼ cup panko bread crumbs

¼ cup grated low fat parmesan cheese

1 tsp garlic powder

1 tsp Italian seasoning

Salt and pepper to taste

1lb. chicken cutlets, skinless, boneless

1 egg, whisked

3 cups green beans

2 tsp. olive oil

½ cup marinara sauce, organic

½ cup fresh low fat mozzarella cheese

¼ cup fresh basil, chopped

Directions

1. Preheat the oven to 4250F. In a mixing bowl, combine the panko breadcrumbs, low fat parmesan cheese, garlic powder, Italian seasoning, salt, and pepper.
2. Soak the chicken breasts into the egg and dredge onto the breadcrumb mixture.
3. Place on a baking sheet. Spray with cooking oil if desired. Toss the beans in olive oil and spread on the baking sheet with the chicken.
4. Allow cooking for 15 minutes, the chicken should be fully cooked through.
5. Remove from the oven and pour the marinara sauce and mozzarella cheese.
6. Return to the oven and cook for 5 minutes or when the low-fat cheese melts. Top with fresh basil.

64. *Shrimp, Basil & Spinach Pasta*

Servings|4   Prep. Time|15 minutes   Cook Time|9 minutes
Nutritional Content (per serving):
Cal|429   Fat|7g   Protein|49g   Carbs|38g

Ingredients:

8 oz uncooked angel hair pasta

1½ tsp olive oil

1½ lbs shrimp, peeled and deveined

3 cloves garlic, minced

Salt and pepper, to taste

2 cups chicken broth, divided

½ tsp dried basil

2 Tbsp lemon juice

2 tsp cornstarch

4 cups fresh spinach, chopped

¼ cup fresh basil, minced

½ cup feta low fat cheese, crumbled

Directions:

1. Cook the pasta according to package directions. Drain and set aside. Set your Instant Pot to Sauté. Add the olive oil. Cook the shrimp for 3 minutes, stirring occasionally. Add the garlic. Season with the salt and pepper. Cook for 1 minute. Transfer the shrimp to a plate.
2. Add half of the broth, basil, and lemon juice. In a bowl, mix together the remaining broth and cornstarch. Add the cornstarch mixture into the pot.. Simmer for 2 minutes. Add the shrimp and spinach. Cook for 3 minutes. Toss the pasta in the shrimp sauce. Top with basil and feta cheese.

65. *Easy Salsa Fish Fillets*

Servings|4   Prep. Time|10 minutes   Cook Time|15 minutes
Nutritional Content (per serving):
Cal|184   Fat|4.3g   Protein|33g   Carbs|2g

Ingredients

4 sole or whitefish fillets

salt and pepper, to taste

1/2 cup bottled salsa (mild or medium)

1/2 cup grated low-fat mozzarella or cheddar cheese

Directions

1. Set your oven to preheat to 425°F. Arrange fish in a single layer on a sprayed lined baking pan. Season.
2. Top each fillet with 2 tablespoons of salsa; sprinkle with cheese. Bake uncovered at 425°F for 10 to 12 minutes, until golden. Fish should flake easily when tested with a fork.

66. *Savoury Roast Turkey Breast*

Servings|4   Prep. Time|10 minutes   Cook Time|1 hour 30 minutes
Nutritional Content (per serving):
Cal|253   Fat|13g   Protein|32g   Carbs|1g

Ingredients:

4 pounds half turkey breast, bone in and skin on

1 ½ teaspoon fresh rosemary

1 teaspoon thyme

1 teaspoon sage, chopped

½ teaspoon salt, divided

1 teaspoon black pepper, plus ½ teaspoon

2 teaspoons lemon zest

2 tablespoons unsalted fat free butter, softened

1 teaspoon extra virgin olive oil

Instructions:

1. Set your oven to preheat to 325°F. Pat dry turkey using paper towels. In a small bowl, combine rosemary, thyme, sage, half of salt, 1 teaspoon pepper, zest, fat free butter, and oil to form a paste. Reserve 1 tablespoon of paste. Rub paste under the skin as far as possible.
2. Rub outside of skin with remaining paste. Season with remaining salt and pepper. Place on rack in roasting pan. Cover with foil, making a tent (sides should be open).
3. Cook 60 to 90 minutes or when your reaches an internal temperature of 165°F. Let rest for 10 to 15 minutes. Slice and serve.

67. *Instant Pot Whole Roast Chicken*

Servings|2   Prep. Time|10 minutes   Cook Time|40 minutes
Nutritional Content (per serving):
Cal|133   Fat|5g   Protein|16g   Carbs|2g

Ingredients

One whole chicken   ½ teaspoon salt
1 tablespoon oil   ½ teaspoon pepper

Directions

1. Set the instant pot on sauté mode and add oil. Place the chicken in the instant pot (breast side down), cook until browned. When done from one side and turn it over and transfer it on a trivet of the pot.
2. Add 1 cup of water at the bottom of the pot. Season chicken with salt and pepper. Cover pot with lid and set instant pot at "Poultry" mode and increase pressure to high. Set timer for 24 minutes.
3. When done, let instant pot pressure release naturally. Carefully open and allow the chicken to rest for about 10 minutes before carving. Serve and enjoy.

68. *Tuna & Ryvita*

Servings|1   Prep. Time|10 minutes   Cook Time|0 minutes
Nutritional Content (per serving):
Cal|253   Fat|3g   Protein|50g   Carbs|8g

Ingredients:

Ryvita crackerbreads (2)   Arugula (70 grams)
Tuna salad (60 grams)   Black pepper (1 tsp, cracked)

Directions:

1. Lay your Ryvita crackerbreads flat on a servings plate. Top with tuna salad, and arugula. Season with black pepper and serve.

69. *Moroccan Sticky Chicken*

Servings|4.6   Prep. Time|10 minutes   Cook Time|10 minutes
Nutritional Content (per serving):
Cal|264   Fat|6.7g   Protein|43g   Carbs|5.2g

Ingredients

Chicken drumsticks (1 lb.)

Paprika (1 tsp.)

Avocado Oil (1 tbsp.)

Garlic powder (1 tsp.)

Cumin (1 tsp., ground)

Ginger (½ tsp., ground)

Cinnamon (½ tsp., ground)

Coriander (¼ tsp., ground)

Saffron threads (¼ tsp. packed)

Salt (1 tsp.)

Black pepper (½ tsp.)

Bone broth (½ cup)

Honey (¼ cup)

Molasses (2 tsp.)

Lemon (1 medium, zest and juiced)

Directions

2. Combine all your spices (paprika, cumin, garlic powder, cinnamon, ginger, saffron, coriander, black pepper, and salt to create a spice rub. Generously coat your chicken with your spice rub and set aside.

3. Allow your instant pot to heat up on 'sauté.' Once hot, use your avocado oil to lightly grease your instant pot.

4. Once the oil is heated, add drumsticks, and cook for about 15 minutes, or until browned on all sides. Add your broth, cover and switch to "manual" and allow to cook for 10 minutes on high pressure.

5. Once the timer goes off, press "keep warm/cancel," and carefully open the steam valve so that its on venting.

Tip: Avoid using natural steam release in this drumstick recipe as it could lead to overcooking.

6. Carefully open and remove the chicken from your instant pot. Cover your drumsticks with aluminum foil and set aside. Set your IP to "Sauté" mode again then keep the lid off.

7. Set your instant pot, with reserved cooking juices, back to sauté and add all your remaining ingredients. Allow to come to a rolling boil, whisking occasionally.

8. Continue to cook for about 5 minutes or when the mixture reduces to a thick sauce (should be able to able to coat a spoon). Hit cancel and serve your drumsticks in your sauce. Enjoy!

Soups, Salads & Snacks

70. *Chicken Soup*

Servings|4   Prep. Time|20 minutes   Cook Time|20 minutes
Nutritional Content (per serving):
Cal| 385   Fat|8 g   Protein|67g   Carbs|8g

Ingredients:

4 up to 5 cups cold water

3 cloves garlic, crushed

2-3 pounds chicken, pastured and free roaming

2 carrots, roughly chopped

2 bay leaves

1/4 radish or turnips, chopped into 2-inch chunks

1 teaspoon black pepper (fresh ground)

1 tablespoon sea salt

1 tablespoon Italian seasoning OR an equal mixture of rosemary (dried), oregano, parsley, and thyme

1 stalk celery, roughly chopped

1 onion (medium), sliced or diced

Purple onion (thinly sliced) or scallion (finely chopped), to garnish

Directions:

1. Put the veggies in your IP. Put the chicken on top and then season the meat with the herbs. Add the water. Lock the lid and close the pressure valve.
2. Set to SOUP for 20 minutes. When the timer beeps, press CANCEL, NPR for 20 up to 30 minutes, then QPR and open the lid.
3. Transfer the meat to a large plate. Remove the meat from the bone. Reserve the bone for bone broth. Return the meat to the pot; stir to mix well.
4. Using the back of a spoon, crush the carrots and celery against the side of the inner pot. Season as needed with pepper and salt. Garnish with scallion or onions and serve.

71. *Healthy Chicken Salad*

Servings|6   Prep. Time|15 minutes   Cook Time|0 minutes
Nutritional Content (per serving):
Cal|195   Fat|9 g   Protein|25g   Carbs|3g

Ingredients

2 cups cooked chicken breasts, chopped
¾ cup non-fat Greek yogurt
¼ cup non-fat sour cream
½ gala apple chopped into small pieces
2 tbsp. bell pepper, minced

1 tbsp. dill pickle relish
1 tsp. garlic powder
1 tsp. onion powder
½ tsp. paprika
½ tsp. black pepper

Directions

1. Combine all your ingredients in a bowl. Serve with crackers if desired.

72. Fennel & Chicken Soup

Servings|6-8   Prep. Time|20 minutes   Cook Time|30 minutes
Nutritional Content (per serving):
Cal|181   Fat|6 g   Protein|25g   Carbs|6g

Ingredients:

1 bay leaf

1 bulb fennel (large), chopped

1 cup kale or spinach, chopped

1 pound chicken breast or/and thighs
(boneless & skinless), sliced into chunks

1 tablespoon oregano (dried)

1/2 onion, chopped

1/8 teaspoon salt

2 cups bone broth (chicken)

3 cloves garlic, peeled & chopped

4 cups water

4 green onions, chopped

Directions:

1. Put everything in your IP. Lock the lid and close the pressure valve. Set to SOUP for 30 minutes. When the timer beeps, press CANCEL, NPR for 10 minutes, then QPR and open the lid. Divide between serving bowls; serve.

73. Chicken Zoodle Soup

Servings|6   Prep. Time|15 minutes   Cook Time|15 minutes
Nutritional Content (per serving):
Cal|57   Fat|1 g   Protein|8g   Carbs|5g

Ingredients:

1-pound chicken breasts, diced

½ cup yellow onion, diced

2 tablespoons olive oil

½ teaspoon thyme, dried

2 garlic cloves, minced

1 cup carrots, diced

1 teaspoon salt

2 zucchinis, spiralized

½ teaspoon turmeric

½ teaspoon oregano

4 cups veggie broth, low-sodium

Directions:

Turn Instant pot to Sauté and set to 10 minutes. Pour olive oil and add diced chicken. Occasionally stir while cooking for 5 minutes then add onion, garlic, carrots, turmeric, herbs and salt. Stir in well then cook for 5 more minutes. Add chicken broth then seal the lid and set to Soup/Broth option, setting the time to 5 minutes. Use Manual release then add spiralized zucchinis. Serve and enjoy.

74. *Lighter Chopped Egg Salad*

Servings|4   Prep. Time|15 minutes   Cook Time|8 minutes
Nutritional Content (per serving):
Cal|49   Fat|2 g   Protein|4g   Carbs|2g

Ingredients

4 hard-boiled eggs

3 tbsp fat-free yogurt

1 stalk celery, minced

2 green onions, minced

1 tbsp minced dill, optional

salt and pepper, to taste

Directions

Cut cooked eggs in half and discard 2 of the yolks (or feed them to your dog). Mash remaining eggs. Mix with remaining ingredients and season to taste.

75. *Classic Chicken Noodle Soup*

Servings|8   Prep. Time|10 minutes   Cook Time|12 minutes
Nutritional Content (per serving):
Cal|170   Fat|5 g   Protein|22g   Carbs|11g

Ingredients:

extra-virgin olive oil 1 tbsp.

1 cup carrots, chopped

1 cup celery, chopped

1 yellow onion, chopped

5 cups chicken broth

3 cups water

1 package of fresh poultry herbs blend (rosemary, sage, and thyme)

Bakers twine

2 bay leaves

1 rotisserie chicken, skin removed and meat pulled from bone (approximately 4 cups)

½ teaspoon garlic powder

½ tsp. salt

½ tsp. black pepper

14 ounces plain Udon noodles, broken into thirds

1 cup fresh parsley, roughly chopped

2 scallions, diced

Directions:

1. In a stock pot or Dutch oven, heat olive oil over medium-high heat. Add carrots, celery, and onions. Sauté until onions are translucent, about 5 minutes.
2. Once vegetables start to soften, add broth and water. Lower heat to medium. Make a bundle out of poultry herbs and tie tightly with the baker's twine.
3. Toss bundle and bay leaves into soup. Add chicken, garlic powder, salt, and pepper to soup.
4. Cover, raise heat to high and allow soup to reach a boil. Once soup has reached a boil, bring
5. to a simmer and cook 5 minutes or when your vegetables are tender. While soup is cooking, prepare Udon noodles according to package directions.
6. When noodles are cooked and drained, divide them among 8 bowls. Remove soup from heat. Remove and discard herb bundle.
7. Stir in parsley. Ladle soup over noodles and garnish with scallions. Serve immediately.

76. *Lighter Chicken Salad*

Servings|6   Prep. Time|15 minutes   Cook Time|0 minutes
Nutritional Content (per serving):
Cal|67   Fat|2.3 g   Protein|9g   Carbs|2g

Ingredients

2 cups cooked, diced or chopped
chicken
1/4 cup minced or grated carrots
2 tbsp minced fresh dill and/or basil (or
1 tsp dried)

2 stalks celery, chopped
4 green onions, chopped
1/2 of a red pepper, chopped
1/3 cup fat-free yogurt
salt and freshly ground pepper, to taste

Directions

1. Combine all ingredients and mix well. To prepare mixture in your processor, remove and discard skin and bones from chicken.
2. Cut chicken and vegetables into large chunks. First, mince carrots and dill using the Steel Knife. Add celery, green onions and red pepper.
3. Process until chopped. Add chicken and process with quick on/offs, until desired texture is reached. Blend in yogurt. Season to taste.

77. *Chicken and Mushroom Soup*

Servings|4   Prep. Time|10 minutes   Cook Time|15 minutes
Nutritional Content (per serving):
Cal|312   Fat|9 g   Protein|45g   Carbs|12g

Ingredients

1 chopped medium leek, white part only

2 cans chicken broth, low sodium

1 cup water

½ teaspoon dried thyme

8 ounces white mushrooms, sliced

chicken breasts, 1 lb., skinless, cut into ½" inch pieces

8 ounces Brussels sprouts, halved

Salt and pepper to taste

Directions

1. Place all Ingredients in a pot. Give a good stir. Close the lid and bring to a boil. Allow to simmer for 15 minutes.

78. *Shrimp and Avocado Lettuce Cups*

Servings|4   Prep. Time|10 minutes   Cook Time|5 minutes
Nutritional Content (per serving):
Cal|326   Fat|11 g   Protein|33g   Carbs|7g

Ingredients

1 tablespoon ghee

½ pound shrimp

½ cup halved grape tomatoes

½ avocado, sliced

4 fat free butter lettuce leaves, rinsed and patted dry

Directions

1. In a medium skillet over medium-high heat, heat the ghee. Add the shrimp and cook. Season with pink salt and pepper.
2. Shrimp are cooked when they turn pink and opaque. Season the tomatoes and avocado with pink salt and pepper.
3. Divide the lettuce cups between two plates. Fill each cup with shrimp, tomatoes, and avocado. Drizzle the mayo sauce on top and serve.

79. *Instant Pot Low Fat Cottage Cheese*

Servings|2 cups   Prep. Time|15 minutes   Cook Time|1 hour 6 minutes
Nutritional Content (per serving):
Cal|98   Fat|4 g   Protein|11g   Carbs|3g

Ingredients:
Low Fat Milk (1 gallon)
Vinegar (3/4 cup, white)

Directions:
1. Add a half of your milk to your instant pot and set the remainder aside. Cover your instant pot and switch your pressure valve to seal. Press the button that says 'yogurt,' then click the 'adjust' button until your instant pot reads 'Boil.'
2. Allow your milk to go through the whole boiling process. When your boiling process ends, adjust the Instant Pot setting so that it is on 'yogurt' mode.
3. Allow to run in this mode for about an hour. Open your instant pot, and slowly add your vinegar and stir. Continue to stir as your milk curdles. Continue to mix until your whey becomes a greenish color and begins to separate from the milk.
4. After you get to this point, use a mesh strainer to strain the whey from the cottage cheese. Discard the whey, and stir in your remaining milk to the low fat cottage cheese until creamy.
5. Pour the mixture into an airtight container. Allow your low fat cottage cheese to rest in the refrigerator until the best by date on the milk container. Enjoy!

80. *Chicken Cordon Bleu Soup*

Servings|4   Prep. Time|5 minutes   Cook Time|3 hours
Nutritional Content (per serving):
Cal|672   Fat|12 g   Protein|70g   Carbs|8g

Ingredients
4 chicken breasts, boneless and skinless
½ cup fat-free milk
1 cup bread stuffing mix

1 can fat-free condensed cream of chicken soup
4 slices lean ham
½ cup blue low fat cheese crumble

Directions
1. Take the chicken soup and milk and mix it, pour it into the slow cooker to cover bottom. Top with chicken.
2. Cover it with the ham, and then ¼ cup of the bleu low fat cheese crumbles. Cover and allow to cook for about 6 hours on low. Enjoy!

81. *Easy Fisherman's Stew*

Servings|4   Prep. Time|20 minutes   Cook Time|2 hours 30 minutes
Nutritional Content (per serving):
Cal|302   Fat|12 g   Protein|45g   Carbs|1g

Ingredients:

6 Tablespoons olive oil

3 large garlic cloves, minced

1 ½ cups chopped onion (about one medium onion)

2/3 cup fresh chopped parsley

1 ½ cups chopped tomato (or use a 14-ounce can of tomatoes, whole or crushed, with their juices)

2 teaspoons tomato paste (optional)

8 oz. of clam juice

½ cup dry white wine

1 ½ lb. firm white fish fillets, cut into 2-inch pieces (good choices are halibut, cod, red snapper, or sea bass)

Pinch of dried oregano

Pinch of dried thyme

1/8 teaspoon Tabasco sauce (or to taste)

Salt and black pepper to taste

Directions

1. In a large heavy pot over medium-high heat, heat olive oil, and add onion. Sauté for about 4 minutes, then add the minced garlic and cook an additional minute.

2. Add parsley, stir for 2 minutes. Stir in tomatoes and tomato paste, and allow to simmer gently for about 10 minutes.

3. Pour in dry white wine and clam juice, then add fish pieces. Return to simmering for about 3 to 5 minutes, until the fish is cooked through and flakes apart easily. Add spices and Tabasco, and salt to taste. Serve in bowls.

82. *Classic Chicken Noodle Soup*

Servings|8   Prep. Time|10 minutes   Cook Time|12 minutes
Nutritional Content (per serving):
Cal|170   Fat|5 g   Protein|22g   Carbs|11g

Ingredients:

extra-virgin olive oil 1 tbsp.

1 cup carrots, chopped

1 cup celery, chopped

1 yellow onion, chopped

5 cups chicken broth

3 cups water

1 package of fresh poultry
herbs blend (rosemary, sage, and
thyme)

Bakers twine

2 bay leaves

1 rotisserie chicken, skin removed
and meat pulled from bone
(approximately 4 cups)

½ teaspoon garlic powder

½ tsp. salt

½ tsp. black pepper

14 ounces plain Udon noodles, broken
into thirds

1 cup fresh parsley, roughly chopped

2 scallions, diced

Directions:

1. Add your olive oil into a stock pot on medium heat. Add carrots, celery, and onions. Sauté until onions are translucent, about 5 minutes. Once vegetables start to soften, add broth and water. Lower heat to medium.
2. Make a bundle out of poultry herbs and tie tightly with the baker's twine. Toss bundle and bay leaves into soup. Add chicken, garlic powder, salt, and pepper to soup.
3. Cover, raise heat to high and allow soup to reach a boil. Once soup has reached a boil, bring
4. to a simmer and cook 5 minutes or when your vegetables are tender. While soup is cooking, prepare Udon noodles according to package directions.
5. When noodles are cooked and drained, divide them among 8 bowls. Remove soup from heat. Remove and discard herb bundle.
6. Stir in parsley. Ladle soup over noodles and garnish with scallions. Serve immediately.

83. *Edamame Beans*

Servings|1   Prep. Time|5 minutes   Cook Time|5 minutes
Nutritional Content (per serving):
Cal|84   Fat|4 g   Protein|8g   Carbs|7g

Ingredients:

Edamame beans (60 grams)   Rock salt – (1 tsp.)

Directions:

1. Set a medium saucepan with salted water over high heat and allow to come to a boil. Once boiling, add edamame beans and cook until tender (about 5 min). Drain, and carefully drop beans out of pods into a medium bowl. Add rock salt and toss to evenly coat. Enjoy!

Serves: 1   **Prep Time: 5 mins.**   **Cook Time:5 mins.**
Calories: 84   **Protein: 8g**   **Carbs: 7g**   **Fat: 4g**

84. *Italian Chopped Salad*

Servings|4   Prep. Time|5 minutes   Cook Time|5 minutes
Nutritional Content (per serving):
Cal|158   Fat|7 g   Protein|5g   Carbs|21g

Ingredients:

8 cups romaine lettuce, washed and rinsed

1 cup chopped tomatoes

1 cup rotini pasta, cooked according to package instruction

2 slices crispy bacon, crumbled

1-ounce cheddar low fat cheese, cut into small cubes

¼ cup fat-free Italian dressing

Directions:

1. Mix all Ingredients in a salad bowl. Toss to coat. Season with salt and pepper if needed. Chill before serving.

85. Healthy Tuna Salad Wraps

Servings|2   Prep. Time|5 minutes   Cook Time|5 minutes
Nutritional Content (per serving):
Cal|272   Fat|6 g   Protein|42g   Carbs|16g

Ingredients:

1 12-ounce can tuna, in water and low-sodium

1 hard-boiled egg, sliced

¼ small onion, chopped

1 tsp dill pickle relish

2 tbsp. Greek yogurt, plain

½ tsp garlic powder

½ tsp black pepper

¼ tsp salt

1 head Bibb lettuce

½ cup tomatoes, halved

Directions:

Drain the water from the tuna. In a bowl, combine the tuna, eggs, onion, pickle, yogurt, garlic powder, black pepper, and salt. Scoop on lettuce leaves and top with tomatoes.

86. Turkey Taco Salad

Servings|5   Prep. Time|10 minutes   Cook Time|10 minutes
Nutritional Content (per serving):
Cal|208   Fat|5 g   Protein|27g   Carbs|17g

Ingredients:

1-pound fat-free ground turkey

1 sweet red pepper, chopped

1 sweet yellow pepper, chopped

1/3 cup chopped onion

1 ½ cups salsa

2 tsp. chili powder

1 tsp ground cumin

8 cups romaine lettuce, torn

10 tortilla chips

5 tbsp. low fat cheddar cheese, grated

Directions:

Heat a non-stick pan over medium flame and stir in the turkey, peppers, and onion. Keep stirring for 6 minutes until the turkey is no longer pink. Stir in the salsa, chili powder, and cumin. Season with salt and pepper to taste. Cook for another 4 minutes. Serve on top of romaine lettuce and garnish with tortilla chips and cheddar cheese.

87. *Faux Caesar Salad*

Servings|5   Prep. Time|5 minutes   Cook Time|5 minutes
Nutritional Content (per serving):
Cal|78   Fat|5 g   Protein|4g   Carbs|5g

Ingredients

2/3 cup non-fat Greek yogurt, plain

1 tbsp red wine vinegar

2 tsp. Dijon mustard

1 tsp Worcestershire sauce

2 tsp. Anchovy paste

10 cups romaine lettuce, washed and drained

30 fresh croutons

2 ½ tbsp. low fat parmesan cheese, grated

Directions

1. In a small bowl, mix the yogurt, red wine vinegar, mustard, and Worcestershire sauce. Shred the romaine lettuce and place in a salad bowl. Top with the salad dressing and mix. Garnish with croutons and parmesan cheese.

Pork Recipes

88. Spinach & Garlic Pork Meatballs

Servings|4-6   Prep. Time|20 minutes   Cook Time|20 minutes
Nutritional Content (per serving):
Cal|287   Fat|13g   Protein|31.7g   Carbs|10g

Ingredients:

1 cup frozen/fresh spinach, chopped

1 pound ground pork (grass-fed)

1/4 cup garlic, minced

4 carrots (large), chopped to 1/2-inch chunks

Preferred bone broth

Real salt & pepper to taste

Directions:

1. Put the carrots and add enough broth to cover them. In a bowl (large), mix the pork, pepper, salt, garlic, and spinach till well mixed, mashing in the process.
2. Roll the meat mixture int0 golf ball-sized pieces.
3. Put the meatballs on top of the carrots. Lock the lid and close the pressure valve.
4. Set to MANUAL for 20 minutes. When the timer beeps, QPR and open the lid.
5. Serve as a soup or serve the meatballs and carrots in a serving dish and the broth in a bowl.

89. *Paleo Egg Roll Soup*

Servings|4   Prep. Time|10 minutes   Cook Time| 2 hours
Nutritional Content (per serving):
Cal|218   Fat|12.9g   Protein|18.7g   Carbs|7.6g

Ingredients:

Avocado oil (1 tbsp.)

Ribbed pork (1 lb.)

2 medium onion (chopped)

Meat broth (5½ cups)

Cabbage (1 ½ lb., chopped)

Carrot (1lb. shredded)

Garlic (1 clove, chopped)

Salt (1 tsp.)

ginger (1 1/2 tsp, ground)

Coconut sauce (3/4 cup)

Cornstarch (3 tbsp.)

Directions:

1. Set your stock pot over medium heat, add your oil and allow to get hot.
2. Once hot, add in your meat then brown on all sides.
3. Add your onions, cabbage, broth, garlic, salt, ginger, and coconut sauce.
4. Cook on low heat for 1 hour and 30 minutes.
5. Combine 3 tbsp. of cornstarch to 2/3 cup of broth together in a small bowl, add to soup, and return to cook (at a low temperature) for another 30 minutes. Serve.

90. *Pork Casserole*

Servings|4   Prep. Time|15 minutes   Cook Time|1 hour 40 minutes
Nutritional Content (per serving):
Cal|400   Fat|10.5g   Protein|28.5g   Carbs|22.5g

Ingredients:

2 Tbsp olive oil

1 lb pork, cut into cubes

2 onions, quarter cut

1 yellow pepper, cut into thick strips

2 red peppers, quarter cut

1 lb ripe tomatoes, quarter cut

2 Tbsp sun-dried tomato paste

2 oz green olives

1 can (2 oz) black olives

2½ cups water

1 cup red wine

6 Tbsp fresh oregano, chopped

Directions:

1. Set a pot on medium heat. Pour the olive oil into the pot. Brown the pork for 5 minutes.
2. Add the onions, yellow peppers, and red peppers. Sauté for 3 minutes. Add the rest of the ingredients, except the fresh oregano.
3. Cover the pot. Cook for an hour and 40 minutes. Garnish with fresh oregano before serving.

91. *Delicious Pork Roast Baracoa*

Servings|10   Prep. Time|10 minutes   Cook Time|8 hours
Nutritional Content (per serving):
Cal|283   Fat|11.7g   Protein|37.1g   Carbs|8g

Ingredients

3 pounds of pork roast, cut into chunks

1 can diced green chilies

6 cloves minced garlic

1 T cumin

2 t salt

Juice from 3 different limes

1 diced onion

2-3 chopped chipotles in adobo sauce

2 T apple cider vinegar

1 T coriander

1 t black pepper

½ cup of fat free pork broth of choice

Directions

1. Take all of your ingredients and put them into the slow cooker, mixing them.
2. Cook on low for 6-8 hours or until your meat can be shredded.
3. Shred the meat and mix with the juices. Serve with a fork for best results.

92. *Swedish Meatballs & Mushrooms Gravy*

Servings|6-8   Prep. Time|15 minutes   Cook Time|40 minutes
Nutritional Content (per serving):
Cal|278   Fat|12.2g   Protein|37g   Carbs|4g

Ingredients:

1 onion (large), chopped

1 pound/ 450 grams ground pork

1 pound/450 grams ground pork

1 teaspoon sage (dried)

1/2 cup coconut milk, bone broth, or water

1/2 teaspoon mace (ground)

1/2 teaspoon sea salt

1/4 cup parsley (fresh), minced, divided

2 cups (cremini/button) mushrooms, sliced

2 tablespoons onion (dried), chopped

3 tablespoons coconut aminos

Directions:

1. In a bowl, mix the pork, pork, salt, mace, dried onion, and 3 tablespoons parsley. Form the mixture into 1-inch meatballs.
2. Put the mushrooms, fresh onion, coconut milk/broth/water, and coconut aminos in your IP. Add the meatballs.
3. Lock the lid and close the pressure valve. Set to MEAT/STEW for 35 minutes. When the timer beeps, QPR and open the lid.
4. Gently transfer the meatballs with a slotted spoon to a serving dish. Using a stick blender or a high-powered blender, puree the remaining contents of the pot.
5. Adding coconut milk/broth/water as needed to thin. Pour the gravy over the meatballs; garnish with the remaining parsley.

NOTES: Serve as an appetizer, main course, over cauliflower rice, or sautéed lectin-free veggies.

93. *Cherry & Apple Pork*

Servings|4   Prep. Time|10 minutes   Cook Time|35 minutes

Nutritional Content (per serving):

Cal|237   Fat|12g   Protein|0.7g   Carbs|6g

Ingredients

olive oil, 1 tbsp., extra virgin, plus some for squash

2 cups dice Apple

⅔ Cup Pit Cherry

⅓ Cup diced Onion

⅓ Cup diced Celery

½ cup Apple Juice, sugar free

⅛ Teaspoon Salt

⅛ Teaspoon Black Pepper

1 ⅓ pounds Boneless Pork Loin

Directions

1. Combine all the ingredients in an Instant Pot and close the lid. Select the Meat/Stew function and cook for 40 minutes.
2. Do a quick release of pressure.

94. *Balsamic Rosemary Pork Tenderloin*

Servings|4   Prep. Time|7 minutes   Cook Time|47 minutes

Nutritional Content (per serving):

Cal|270   Fat|8.25g   Protein|44.7g   Carbs|1.4g

Ingredients:

1 1/2 pounds quarter pork tenderloin

1 1/2 teaspoons balsamic vinegar

1 cup water, for the IP

1 teaspoon rosemary, dried

1 teaspoon salt (kosher)

1/4 teaspoons black pepper (fresh ground)

2 teaspoons olive oil

4 teaspoons minced garlic, cloves

Directions:

1. Mix the garlic, pepper, salt, and rosemary in a bowl. Massage the pork with the seasonings. Whisk the olive oil and balsamic vinegar.
2. Put the IP trivet and pour 1 cup water in the inner pot. Put the pork on the trivet. Pour the oil mixture on top of the meat.
3. Lock the lid and close the pressure valve. Set to HIGH pressure for 20 minutes.
4. When the timer beeps, press CANCEL, NPR completely, then QPR and open the lid. Serve.

95. *Paleo Italian Pork*

Servings|4   Prep. Time|5 minutes   Cook Time|2 hours 45 minutes
Nutritional Content (per serving):
Cal|288   Fat|11g   Protein|42g   Carbs|1.6g

Ingredients

3 lbs. grass-fed pork roast, cut into pieces

1 tablespoons garlic powder

1 tsp onion powder

1 teaspoon ginger powder

1 teaspoon oregano

1 teaspoon basil

1 teaspoons salt

2½ cup chicken broth

14 tablespoons apple cider vinegar

Directions

1. In a bowl add garlic powder, onion powder, ginger powder, oregano, basil, and salt. Stir to fully incorporate.
2. Rub this mixture on your roast and set aside. Set a deep pot on medium heat. Once hot add your roast and allow to brown on all sides evenly (about 2 minutes per side).
3. Drizzle pork broth and apple cider vinegar into the pot. Cover with lid, set to cook on low heat for 2 hours and 45 minutes.
4. Remove pork roast from pot. Add your meat into a shallow platter.
5. Pull the meat apart using two forks. To do this use the first fork to hold the meat steady by stabbing it directing in the center of the meat.
6. Next, place the second fork into the meat where the first fork is, with the teeth facing you, then pull it towards you.
7. Repeat this process until you have shredded all the pork. Serve, and enjoy.

96. *Corned Pork*

Servings|6   Prep. Time|5 minutes   Cook Time|2 hours 30 minutes
Nutritional Content (per serving):
Cal|379.2   Fat|10.6g   Protein|59.1g   Carbs|9.7g

Ingredients

3-pounds corned pork brisket

2 cups red potatoes, whole

1 onion, halved

9-10 garlic cloves

5½ cups of pork broth

1 cabbage, chopped

1 bay leaf

2 cloves

12-15 peppercorns

2 tablespoons coriander seeds

¼ teaspoon cumin seeds

2 cinnamon sticks

2 tablespoons cornstarch

Directions

1. Transfer pork to a deep pot with onion, red potatoes, pork broth, all spices, and garlic. Cover.
2. Cook over a medium flame for 2 hours and 20 minutes. When done, add cabbage into the pot and cook on a high flame for few minutes or until the cabbage is cooked.
3. After that remove pork and vegetables from your pot, leaving drippings.
4. Mix cornstarch with drippings until combined. Now whisk this mixture into the pork juices and cook it on medium flame till boiled.
5. Reduce flame and cook for 3-4 minutes more. Serve and enjoy.

97. *Chipotle Pork Carnitas*

Servings|8   Prep. Time|15 minutes   Cook Time|2 hours 45 minutes
Nutritional Content (per serving):
Cal|172   Fat|4.1g   Protein|30.2g   Carbs|2g

Ingredients

pork shoulder, blade roast, 2 lb.,
boneless and trimmed
1/2 tsp garlic powder
dry adobo seasoning, 1/4 tsp
2 bay leaves
2 chipotle peppers
1¾ cup chicken stock

Oregano, 1/4 tsp, dried
2 tsp salt
1/2 tsp sazon
1 tsp cumin
5 garlic cloves, cut into slivers
Black pepper to taste

Directions

1. In a large pan, brown the pork on all sides over the high heat for 5 minutes. Remove pork from pan and set aside to cool.
2. Place a knife about an inch into your pork then insert garlic slivers, do this all over.
3. Season pork using garlic powder, adobo, oregano, sazon and cumin. Pour chicken stock in your pot.
4. Stir in chipotle peppers and bay leaves then place pork in a deep pot. Cover and set to cook for 2 hours and 40 minutes over low heat.
5. Shred pork using forks and combine with juices.
6. Remove bay leaves and mix well. Serve hot and enjoy.

98. *Balsamic Roast Pork*

Servings|5-10   Prep. Time|5-10 minutes   Cook Time|1 hour
Nutritional Content (per serving):
Cal|321   Fat|11g   Protein|44g   Carbs|9g

Ingredients:

1 1/2 teaspoon truffle salt or salt

1 cup pork broth

1 tablespoon coconut aminos

1 tablespoon fish sauce

1 tablespoon honey

1 tablespoon olive oil (extra-virgin)

1/2 cup balsamic vinegar

1/2 teaspoon rosemary and/or lavender (dried), optional

3-4 pounds shoulder or pork roast

4 cloves garlic, crushed

Directions:

1. Pat dry the roast using paper towels; rub all the sides of the pork with the salt. Put the olive oil in the IP.
2. Set the IP to SAUTE. Add the roast; sear each side for 2-3 minutes or till brown.
3. Add the rest of the ingredients in the pot. Lock the lid and close the pressure valve.
4. Set to HIGH pressure for 45 minutes. Transfer the roast to a serving dish; tent with foil and let rest for 5 up to 10 minutes.
5. Meanwhile, set the IP to SAUTE. Cook the juices in the pot for about 10 minutes or till reduced to about 2/3; keep an eye on it.
6. Slice the roast and drizzle the sauce over it. Garnish with salt and parsley.

99. *Slow Cooked Pork Tenderloin*

Servings|6   Prep. Time|5 minutes   Cook Time|8 hours
Nutritional Content (per serving):
Cal|264   Fat|6.4g   Protein|40.6g   Carbs|8.3g

Ingredients

2 pounds of pork tenderloin

½ cup low sodium chicken broth

2 tbsp. stevia

½ tsp. garlic powder and cumin

Salt and pepper for taste

¼ cup balsamic vinegar

2 tbsp. soy sauce

¼ tsp. chili powder

Directions

1. Add your soy sauce and vinegar to your slow cooker then stir to combine.
2. Add your remaining and spoon some of your vinegar mixture on top of the pork. Close the lid and allow to cook until very tender, usually about 6-8 hours.
3. If you want, you can reduce the cooking liquid to create a nice glaze. If you want a crisper outside, put it in a broiler for at least 4-5 minutes.

100. *Corned Pork w/ Cabbage & Carrots*

Servings|12   Prep. Time|15 minutes   Cook Time|1 hour, 15 minutes
Nutritional Content (per serving):
Cal|317   Fat|9.7g   Protein|47.3g   Carbs|8.1g

Ingredients:

1 cup (around 2 pieces) 2 onions, sliced

1 cup (around 4 pieces) carrots, sliced into thirds

1 cup (around 4 stalks) celery, chopped

1 head cabbage, cut into wedges (8 cups)

2 teaspoons black peppercorns (fresh ground)

2 teaspoons mustard (dried)

4 cloves garlic

4 pounds corned pork brisket

6 cups water

Directions:

1. Put the pork in your IP; discard the spice packet that is packed with the meat.
2. Add the water to the pot; adding more as needed to cover the pork. Add the spices.
3. Lock the lid and close the pressure valve. Set to MEAT/STEW HIGH pressure for 60 minutes.
4. When the timer beeps, press CANCEL, NPR completely, then QPR and open the lid. Transfer the pork to a serving dish; cover with foil to keep warm.
5. Add the veggies to the IP. Lock the lid and close the pressure valve. Set to SOUP for 15 minutes.
6. When the timer beeps, QPR and open the lid. Return the pork to the pot; let warm. Serve.

101. *Pork with Carrots & Apples*

Servings|4   Prep. Time|10 minutes   Cook Time|10 minutes
Nutritional Content (per serving):
Cal|337   Fat|6g   Protein|33g   Carbs|11g

Ingredients

4 ½ boneless skinless pork loins (about ½ inch thick or 4 ounces each)

1 tablespoon of extra virgin olive oil, divided

1 teaspoon ground ginger

½ teaspoon ground sage

¼ teaspoon freshly ground

black pepper

1 tablespoon unsalted fat free butter

1 large apple (Pink Lady works well), peeled, cored and cubed

1 cup diced carrots (approximately 5 5 small)

¼ cup water

Directions

1. Rub half the olive oil on all sides of pork. Mix ginger, sage, and pepper together and rub on both sides of pork chops.
2. Heat the other half of the oil in a large skillet over medium heat. Add pork to the skillet and sauté until brown, about 3 to 4 minutes per side and then transfer to a platter.
3. Add fat free butter, chopped apple, and carrots to the skillet and sauté until golden brown.
4. Stir in approximately ¼ cup of water and cook until tender. Add pork to the skillet and simmer until hot.

102. Shredded Pork Tacos

Servings|11   Prep. Time|10 minutes   Cook Time|2 hours 45 minutes
Nutritional Content (per serving):
Cal|130   Fat|7g   Protein|20g   Carbs|1g

Ingredients

2 ½ lbs. pork shoulder roast (trimmed, boneless)
6 garlic cloves (sliced)
1 ½ teaspoons cumin
¼ teaspoon oregano (dry)
2 teaspoons salt
2 bay leaves
¼ teaspoon adobo seasoning (dry)
½ teaspoon garlic powder

2 chipotle peppers (placed in adobo sauce)
½ teaspoon sazon
Black pepper, to taste
1¾ cups chicken broth (reduced-sodium)
Romaine lettuce leaves (enough to serve)

Directions

1. Season the pork with salt and pepper and brown it in a pot set over medium heat for 5 minutes.
2. Using a knife out incisions on the pork and push garlic pieces in. Rub the oregano, adobo seasoning, cumin, sazon and garlic powder over the pork.
3. Replace the pork to the pot and add the rest of the ingredients. Cover and set to cook for 2 hours and 40 minutes on low heat or until fully cooked.
4. Shred the pork using forks and add back to the pot.
5. Discard the bay leaves. Serve in warm Romaine lettuce leaves.

103. *Pork Ragu with Tagliatelle*

Servings|4   Prep. Time|5 minutes   Cook Time|50 minutes
Nutritional Content (per serving):
Cal|363   Fat|8.9g   Protein|25.7g   Carbs|8.9g

Ingredients

9 oz. Tagliatelle

14 oz. extra lean minced pork

14 oz. tomatoes, chopped

4 garlic cloves, chopped

2 carrots, finely diced

2 celery sticks, chopped

1 finely chopped onion

2 tablespoons tomato puree

1 teaspoon olive oil

½ teaspoon dried oregano

½ teaspoon stevia

1 bay leaf

2 cups water

Salt and pepper, to taste

Directions

1. Heat oil in a large non-stick frying pan, add minced pork and cook on a high heat for 5 minutes, stirring and breaking the meat up as it cooks.
2. Transfer cooked meat into a large saucepan, heat more olive oil in the frying pan and add carrots, onion and celery and cook over a low heat for 10 minutes, add a splash of water if required.
3. Stir in garlic and oregano and continue to cook for another 2 minutes, transfer the mixture into your saucepan. Add stevia, bay leaf and water.
4. Season with salt and pepper and bring to a boil, simmer for 45 minutes stirring occasionally until you have a rich and thick sauce.
5. Once your ragu is ready, cook pasta in accordance with the instructions on the packet and drain.
6. Divide into bowls and top with sauce.

104. *Crock Pot Asian Pork with Mushrooms*

Servings|7   Prep. Time|20 minutes   Cook Time|8 hours
Nutritional Content (per serving):
Cal|224.4   Fat|8.5g   Protein|25g   Carbs|11g

Ingredients

pork sirloin roast, 2 lb., lean, boneless

salt and fresh cracked pepper

non-stick oil spray

chicken broth, 1 cup, fat-free, low-sodium

soy sauce, ½ cup, low sodium

balsamic vinegar, 1/ 3 cup

Stevia, 3 tbsp.

Cayenne and sesame oil, 1 tsp.

Chinese five spice, ½ tsp.

Garlic, 3 cloves, crushed

ginger root, 1 tbsp., grated

mushrooms, 8 oz., sliced

For Topping:

Scallions, ¼ cup, chopped

Cilantro, ¼ cup, chopped

Directions

1. Season the pork. Heat a skillet on medium-high heat spray with a little oil and brown pork for about 7-8 minutes.
2. Add your ginger, garlic, five spice, sesame oil, agave, vinegar, soy sauce and broth into your slow cooker.
3. Toss in the pork then set to low and cook for 8 hours. Take the pork out with 30 minutes before the time ends and allow the pork to rest.
4. Toss in your mushrooms, cover and cook for about 30 minutes. Shred the pork and set to the side to re add once your mushrooms are cooked.
5. Once the mushrooms have been cooked remove a cup of the broth and add in your pork and mix.
6. Add your spinach at the very end, cover until it wilts. Serve.

105. *Pork with Olives & Feta*

Servings|4   Prep. Time|10 minutes   Cook Time|1 hour
Nutritional Content (per serving):
Cal|378   Fat|9g   Protein|36g   Carbs|14g

Ingredients:

2 lb pork stew meat, cubed

30 oz spicy diced tomatoes with juice

½ cup black olives

½ cup green olives

½ tsp salt

¼ tsp black pepper

4 cups cooked rice

Directions:

1. Put the pork, tomatoes, black olives and green olives in the Instant Pot. Season with salt and pepper.
2. Seal the pot. Turn to Manual. Cook on high for 1 hour. Top with the feta cheese.
3. Serve with rice.

106. *Pork & Broccoli*

Servings|4   Prep. Time|20 minutes   Cook Time|30 minutes
Nutritional Content (per serving):
Cal|267   Fat|7.5g   Protein|37.9g   Carbs|9.3g

Ingredients:

1 clove garlic, (large), crushed/pressed

1 onion, quartered

1 pound stewing pork meat

1 teaspoon ginger (ground)

1/2 cup pork/bone broth

1/2 teaspoon salt

1/4 cup coconut aminos

10-12 ounces frozen broccoli (bagged)

2 tablespoons fish sauce

Directions:

1. Except for your broccoli, put the rest of your ingredients in the IP. Lock the lid and close the pressure valve.
2. Set the MEAT/STEW and cook on preset cooking time. When the timer beeps, QPR and open the lid. Add the broccoli.
3. Loosely cover the IP with the lid; let sit for 15 minutes or till the broccoli is cooked to the desired doneness with the residual heat. Serve.

107. _Bone in Ham with Maple-Honey Glaze_

Servings|14   Prep. Time|5 minutes   Cook Time|1 hour 15 minutes
Nutritional Content (per serving):
Cal|60   Fat|1g   Protein|10g   Carbs|3g

Ingredients

8 tablespoons Maple Syrup
4 tablespoons honey
1½ cups Orange Juice

1 cup pineapple juice, sugar free
2 cinnamon sticks
1 Bone-In Ham

Directions

1. Create a glaze by combining your maple syrup, honey, orange juice, pineapple juice, and cinnamon together in a saucepan over medium heat. Mix well and allow to cook until the mixture thickens.
2. Remove from heat and set aside. Add your ham into a deep pot, cover and set to cook over medium heat for 50 minutes.
3. Transfer ham into oven safe dish and drizzle over glaze. Place under broiler till glaze is caramelized. Serve and enjoy.

108. *Spicy Pork Pot Roast*

Servings|8   Prep. Time|20 minutes   Cook Time|2 hours 30 minutes
Nutritional Content (per serving):
Cal|302   Fat|12 g   Protein|45g   Carbs|1g

Ingredients:

2 medium dried ancho chilis, stem and seeds removed

3 medium dried guajillo chilis, stem and seeds removed

2 bay leaves

2 Tablespoons cider vinegar

1 small yellow or white onion, coarsely chopped

3 cloves garlic, chopped

1 tsp thyme, marjoram or oregano (ideally a mix of all three)

1/4 tsp fresh ground allspice

1/4 tsp fresh ground cloves

1 1/2 Tablespoons vegetable oil

1/2 tsp Salt

3 1/2 lbs. boneless pork shoulder or butt roast, or bone-in pork shoulder roast with some skin left on

Directions

1. Place the chilis in a small bowl, fill with hot water and let stand for 10-20 minutes to rehydrate. Put a heavy cup on top of the chilis to keep them submerged.
2. Transfer the chilis plus a cup of liquid to the blender. Grind the spices in a spice grinder, then add to the blender along with the vinegar, onion, garlic, and mixed herbs. Process to a smooth puree.
3. With a boneless cut, slice into 3 inches thick slabs. Place the roast in a large roasting pot and spoon or rub the chili paste all over, working into the incisions.
4. Pour the remaining cup of water around the meat, cover, bring to a boil, and simmer for about 2 1/2 hours.
5. Let the pork stand, covered, for about 20 minutes before serving. The meat should be fork tender. Remove the bone, shred, and serve.

109. *Pork Roasted Carnitas*

Servings|11   Prep. Time|15 minutes   Cook Time|8 hours
Nutritional Content (per serving):
Cal|161   Fat|5 g   Protein|28g   Carbs|1g

Ingredients

3 pounds of trimmed, boneless shoulder blade roast

Black pepper for taste

2 t cumin

¼ t dry oregano

2-3 chipotle peppers in adobo sauce, more to taste

¼ t dry adobo seasoning

2 t salt

6 cloves of garlic, slivered

½ tsp. sazon

1 cup reduced sodium chicken broth

2 bay leaves

Directions

1. Season the pork and sauté it on medium high heat for about 10 minutes, browning the sides.
2. Let it cool. Insert knife into pork and put the garlic slivers in there, pushing it all the way in so you don't' see them. season with the cumin, sazon, adobo, and oregano all over your meat.
3. Put it in the slow cooker and put the bay leaves and the peppers in there. Cook it on low for about 8 hours.
4. You can then combine it with the juices that you have and add more seasonings, letting it cook for another 15 minutes if you so desire.

110. *Brown Stewed Pork*

Servings|1   Prep. Time|5 minutes   Cook Time|45 minutes
Nutritional Content (per serving):
Cal|120   Fat|7 g   Protein|14g   Carbs|0g

Ingredients

Thyme (1 sprig)   Onion (1, small, diced)
Bay Leaf (1 dry)   Carrot (1, small, diced)
Cloves (2, whole)   Celery (1 stalk, diced)
Kitchen twine   Tomato Paste (1 Tbsp.)
Pork (2lbs, trimmed)   White Wine (1 Cup, dry)
Sea salt and pepper (1 tsp each)   Pork Stock (3 Cups)
Vegetable oil (1/2 Cup)   Parsley (3 Tbsp., chopped)

Directions:

1. Create a bouquet garni by tying your cheesecloth with the thyme, rosemary, cloves, and bay leaf cloves inside then secure it with a piece of twine.
2. Use a piece of paper towel to remove the excess moisture from the pork pieces in a patting motion. Season with salt and pepper.
3. Heat the oil in your Dutch oven pot until it begins to smoke. Set your pork to brown on all sides. Remove the pork pieces from the heat and set aside.
4. In the pot, you took the pork from, pour in the carrots, onion, and celery then add salt to season. Sauté for about 8 minutes or when your completely soft.
5. Mix in the tomato paste to the carrot mixture in the pot and add browned pork. Pour in the white wine and allow it to cook until the liquid is reduced by half.
6. Pour in the 2 cups of the stock along with the bouquet garni and allow boiling. Cover the pot, set the heat to low and simmer until the meat is literally falling off the bone when lifted.
7. Ensure that the liquid is about ¾ way up the pork by checking on it in 15-minute intervals. When the meat has cooked remove the pork from the pot and plate in preparation to serve.
8. Remove and discard the kitchen twine and the bouquet garni. Use the juices from the pot to pour over the pork pieces. Serve and Enjoy!

111. *Slow-Cooked Tender Pot Roast & Holy Grail Gravy*

Servings|4-8   Prep. Time|15 minutes   Cook Time|6-8 hours
Nutritional Content (per serving):
Cal|296   Fat|9 g   Protein|43g   Carbs|10g

Ingredients:

1 bay leaf (whole)

1 onion (chopped)

1/4 cup broth or water

2 (whole) branches rosemary (fresh)

2 stalks celery, thickly sliced

2-4 garlic cloves (whole)

2-4 pounds pork roast (bone-out or bone-in)

4 carrots, chopped into chunks

Black pepper (fresh ground), optional

Sea salt

Directions:

1. Put all the vegetables and herbs in your IP. Add 1/4 cup of broth. Season all the sides of the roast with pepper and salt. Put it on top of the veggies.
2. Lock the lid and close the pressure valve. Set to SLOW COOK NORMAL mode for 6 up to 8 hours.
3. When the timer beeps, QPR and open the lid. The meat is done when it is easily shredded with a fork.
4. Transfer the pork to a plate. Remove the rosemary and bay leaf; discard them. Transfer the cooking liquid to a blender. Add 1/2 of the cooked veggies; puree till smooth.
5. Add more veggies to thicken and strengthen the flavor of the gravy as needed. Season with pepper and salt to taste.
6. Serve the roast with the gravy, and with mashed garlic cauliflower.

112. *Italian Pork*

Servings|6   Prep. Time|5 minutes   Cook Time|2 hours 5 minutes
Nutritional Content (per serving):
Cal|279   Fat|9 g   Protein|44g   Carbs|4g

Ingredients:

1 cup pork broth

1 teaspoon basil

1 teaspoon marjoram

1 teaspoon onion powder

1 teaspoon oregano

1 teaspoon salt (Himalayan pink)

1/2 teaspoon ginger (ground)

1/4 cup vinegar (apple cider)

2 teaspoons garlic powder

3 pounds pork roast (grass-fed)

6 cloves garlic

Directions:

1. With a sharp knife, preferably pairing, cut 6 slits in the meat; stuff each with 1 garlic cloves. Whisk the salt, marjoram, basil, oregano, ginger, onion powder, and garlic powder till well mixed.
2. Rub all the sides of the roast with the spice rub. Put in the IP.
3. Add the broth and the vinegar. Lock the lid and close the pressure valve. Set to MANUAL to 90 minutes. When the timer beeps, press CANCEL, NPR for 20 minutes, then QPR and open the lid.
4. Transfer the pork to a large plate or cutting board; shred using caveman claws or 2 forks. Moisten with some of the cooking juice if desired.

113. *Pork Noodle & Mushroom*

Servings|4   Prep. Time|15 minutes   Cook Time|8 hours
Nutritional Content (per serving):
Cal|264   Fat|6 g   Protein|41g   Carbs|8g

Ingredients

½ lb. Portobello mushrooms

1 lb. pork steak, cubed

2 T olive oil

2 cups pork broth

2 T cornstarch

2 cups cooked egg noodles

1 sliced onion

½ t salt

¼ cup red wine

1 T Worcestershire sauce

¼ cup cold water

Directions

1. Put the onions and mushrooms into the slow cooker. Season the pork to taste. Brown the pork on high in a skillet with oil. Put meat in slow cooker and use wine and about 1/3 of the broth that pork was in to deglaze it.
2. Put the broth and the Worcestershire sauce together until mixed, adding it to the slow cooker. Allow to cook for about 8 hours on low.
3. Put the cornstarch and water together and then put it into the slow cooker for about 15-30 minutes, or until it's reached the right consistency.
4. Cook the egg noodles, and then serve the pork tips with the mushroom gravy and the egg noodles for best results.

114. *Spicy Braised Pork*

Servings|9   Prep. Time|10 minutes   Cook Time|3 hours
Nutritional Content (per serving):
Cal|153   Fat|5 g   Protein|24g   Carbs|10g

Ingredients

5 garlic cloves

1 onion (medium)

1 lime (juiced)

2 tablespoons chipotles in adobo sauce

2 tablespoons oregano

2 tablespoons cumin

1/2 teaspoon cloves

2½ cup water

3 lbs pork, trimmed, chopped into 3"
pieces

2½ teaspoons salt

Black pepper

2 teaspoons oil

3 bay leaves

Directions

1. Combine the cloves, water, chipotle, oregano, lime juice, cumin, onion and garlic in a blender and blend until smooth. Season the meat with salt and pepper then brown in a deep pot with oil over medium heat.
2. Pour in the blended sauce, and mix in the bay leaves. Cover and all to come to a boil. Switch to low heat and cook for 3 hours or until pork is fully cooked.
3. Remove the meat and shred it. Mix the shredded meat with 1 ½ cups of the cooking liquid.

115. *Oven Fried Pork Chops*

Servings|6   Prep. Time|20 minutes   Cook Time|30 minutes
Nutritional Content (per serving):
Cal|378   Fat|13 g   Protein|33g   Carbs|8g

Ingredients:

pork chops, 6, boneless, fat trimmed

salt

egg, 1 large, beaten

black pepper, 1/ 8 tsp

panko crumbs, ½ cup

sweet paprika, 1 ¼ tsp.

cornflakes, 1/ 3 cup, crushed

Low fat parmesan cheese, 2 tbsp., grated

garlic powder, ½ tsp.

chili powder, ¼ tsp.

onion powder, ½ tsp.

Directions:

1. Set your oven to preheat to 425 and lightly grease your baking sheet. Season pork chops with salt. Combine pepper, chili powder, onion powder, garlic powder, paprika, salt, low fat parmesan cheese, cornflakes and panko.
2. Place beaten egg in another. Dredge your pork into your eggs then directly into the bowl of crumbs. Transfer your chops to a baking sheet.
3. Lightly spray a little more oil on top of the pork and bake in the oven for 30 minutes.

116. *Spicy Green Chili Pork*

Servings|2   Prep. Time|10 minutes   Cook Time|8 hours
Nutritional Content (per serving):
Cal|215   Fat|8 g   Protein|16g   Carbs|5g

Ingredients

1 Onion Salt and Pepper
2 ½ Lb. Pork Shoulder Roast
1 16 oz. Jar Green Salsa

½ C. Chopped Cilantro, Fresh
2 Serrano Chile Peppers

Directions

1. Layer the onions in the bottom of the slow cooker and season the pork shoulder with salt and pepper.
2. Place the pork shoulder on top of the onions and pour the green salsa over top. Sprinkle the cilantro over the pork and add in your peppers.
3. Continue to cook until the meat is fully cooked, about eight hours. Transfer the pork to a cutting board then toss out the liquid from the pot.
4. Then discard the onions and peppers. Shred the pork and mix it with the reserved liquid before serving.

117. *Lancaster County Pork and Sauerkraut*

Servings|2   Prep. Time|20 minutes   Cook Time|6 hours
Nutritional Content (per serving):
Cal|392   Fat|9 g   Protein|37g   Carbs|4g

Ingredients:

1 4lb. Pork Loin Roast
1 tsp. Caraway Seeds Salt and Pepper

2 C. Sauerkraut

Directions

Cut the loin if you need to in order to fit it into the slow cooker. Season it with the caraway seeds, salt and pepper to your taste. Add your sauerkraut on your roast then set to cook for 1 hour on high. Switch to low heat and continue to cook for about 6 hours.

Desserts

118. *Brownie Cake*

Servings|4   Prep. Time|10 minutes   Cook Time|40 minutes
Nutritional Content (per serving):
Cal|112   Fat|7g   Protein|1.5g   Carbs|12g

Ingredients

Fat free butter (4 tbsp., unsalted)

Chocolate chips (2 tbsp., stevia-sweetened)

Stevia (⅔ cup)

Eggs (2)

Vanilla (¼ tsp., extract)

Whole wheat flour (½ cup)

Cocoa powder (4 tbsp., unsweetened)

Directions

1. Set your oven to preheat to 300 degrees F. Add your chocolate chips, and fat free butter in a small microwave safe bowl and place in the microwave to heat for 1 minute on high so that they melt.
2. Stir, and add it to a large mixing bowl. To your mixing bowl, add your stevia, and whisk to combine.
3. Add your vanilla and eggs and continue whisking until fully blended. Sift all your dry ingredients into your wet ingredients and fold in with a wooden spoon to fully combine.
4. Spoon your batter into multiple ramekins and set aside.
5. Add 2 cups of water to a hotel pan. Carefully place your ramekins into the water and cover the hotel pan with a layer of aluminum foil.
6. Set your hotel pan in your preheated oven and allow to steam for 45 minutes or until your brownie cake is done. Enjoy.

119. *Apple Crisp*

Servings|4   Prep. Time|15 minutes   Cook Time|35 minutes
Nutritional Content (per serving):
Cal|161   Fat|3.4g   Protein|1.8g   Carbs|31g

Ingredients

Apple (5 medium)   Fat free butter (4 tbsp., melted)
Cinnamon (2 tsp)   Rolled oats (3/4 cup, old fashioned)
Nutmeg (1/2 tsp.)   Flour (1/4 cup, whole wheat)
Water (1/2 cup)   Stevia (1/4 cup)
Maple syrup (1 tbsp.)   Salt (1/2 tsp.)

Directions

1. Set your oven to preheat to 375 degrees F. Wash your apples then remove the core, stem, and seeds. Cut each cored apple into quarters and add to a greased baking dish.

2. Top with your nutmeg, cinnamon, maple syrup, and water. In a separate bowl, combine your salt, stevia, flour, oats, and fat free butter; stir well to combine. Spoon this mixture evenly over the apples.

3. Set to bake into your preheated oven until golden (about 35 minutes). Once done, remove from oven and allow to rest for 10 minutes.

4. Serve, and enjoy!

120. *Tapioca Pudding*

Servings|4.6   Prep. Time|15 minutes   Cook Time|35 minutes
Nutritional Content (per serving):
Cal|187   Fat|2.7g   Protein|2.5g   Carbs|39.5g

Ingredients

Tapioca pearls (⅓ cup, rinsed and drained)

Coconut Milk (1¼ cups)

Water (½ cup)

Stevia (1/4 cup)

Vanilla bean (½, seeds only)

Directions

1. Pour 2½ cups of water into a deep pot and fit a steamer basket to the bottom. Set aside.
2. In a heat proof bowl, combine your stevia, vanilla beans, water, milk, and tapioca then mix well.
3. Place your bowl into your pot. Cover, and set to cook on medium heat for about 35 minutes.
4. Cautiously transfer your heat-proof bowl to a cooling rack. Vigorously stir then pour evenly into serving vessels.
5. Plastic wrap tightly and chill for at least 3 hours before serving. Enjoy!

121. *Walnut Cake*

Servings|12.15   Prep. Time|15 minutes   Cook Time|40 minutes
Nutritional Content (per serving):
Cal|180   Fat|7g   Protein|2g   Carbs|28g

Ingredients:

3½ cups whole wheat flour

¼ teaspoon baking powder

2 teaspoons baking soda

½ cup stevia

4 large eggs

1½ cups fat free buttermilk

½ cup fat free butter, softened

1 teaspoon vanilla

½ teaspoon salt

1½ cups walnuts, finely ground

½ cup vegetable oil

frosting

Directions:
1. Heat oven to 350 degrees and lightly grease a baking dish. In a bowl, combine salt, baking powder, flour and baking soda; set aside.
2. In another bowl, beat fat free butter, oil and stevia together until smooth; beat in eggs individually, then vanilla.
3. Add flour mixture to egg mixture alternately with fat free buttermilk, beating just until smooth and blended fold in ground walnuts.
4. Pour batter into your baking dish and set to bake for about 35 minutes, or until toothpick can be inserted in the center and come out clean. Cool; frost.

122. *Fat free buttermilk Prune Muffins*

Servings|12   Prep. Time|15 minutes   Cook Time|30 minutes
Nutritional Content (per serving):
Cal|194.9   Fat|3.8g   Protein|3.8g   Carbs|121g

Ingredients:

2 cups water

1 cup prune bits

5 tablespoons fat free butter, softened

3 tablespoons stevia

2 eggs, lightly beaten

1 cup fat free buttermilk, room temperature

½ teaspoon salt

½ teaspoon lemon peel powder

½ teaspoon cinnamon

¾ cup whole wheat flour

1¼ cup all-purpose or light baking flour

1 tablespoon baking powder

½ teaspoon baking soda

Directions:

1. Heat oven to 400 degrees. In a small saucepan, boil water; remove from heat. Add prunes and let soak for 8 minutes.
2. Drain prunes; sift some of the flour over the prune bits; toss to coat, then set aside.
3. In a large bowl, cream fat free butter and stevia; add eggs and fat free buttermilk.
4. Add salt, lemon powder, cinnamon, flours, baking powder and baking soda, mixing just until the dry ingredients are moistened, and a few lumps remain; fold in prunes.
5. Spoon batter into greased muffin cups; bake at 400 degrees for 18 minutes, or until toothpick inserted in center comes out clean.

123. *Bohemian Apple Kolaches*

Servings|6   Prep. Time|15 minutes   Cook Time|1 hour 40 minutes
Nutritional Content (per serving):
Cal|60.4   Fat|4.2g   Protein|0.7g   Carbs|5g

Ingredients:

2 packages active dry yeast
½ cup plus 1 tablespoon stevia
¼ cup lukewarm water
1¼ cups fat free butter, divided, melted
2 cups almond milk
2 whole eggs plus 4 yolks
1 ½ teaspoons salt

½ teaspoon powdered lemon peel
1 teaspoon vanilla
6 – 7 cups whole wheat flour
Apple Filling
2 cups applesauce
1 egg, beaten, reserved
cinnamon and stevia mixed

Directions:

1. Heat oven to 400 degrees. Dissolve yeast in ¼ cup lukewarm water; add 1 tablespoon stevia, stir.
2. Rest yeast mixture for 5 minutes or when your bubbly. Meanwhile, combine 1 cup melted fat free butter and almond milk in the microwave or a saucepan until warmed (not scalding).
3. In a large bowl, add whole eggs and yolks plus remaining stevia and beat until thickened.
4. Add almond milk and fat free butter mixture to egg mixture; beat in salt, lemon peel and vanilla. Beat in flour, one cup at a time, until it becomes too thick to beat.
5. Place dough on floured pastry board and knead until smooth, about 5 minutes. Place in greased bowl, rounding up with greased side up.
6. Place a towel on top of the dough and place to double in a warm place. Punch down dough; place on a lightly floured board and divide into 6 large pieces.
7. Next cut each of the large pieces into 12 smaller pieces; form each into balls.
8. Place balls on a baking sheet and brush each with melted fat free butter; cover and let rise again until double.
9. Press the center of each down, making a flat indentation in the center, and fill each with 1 tablespoon applesauce; let rise again, about 30 minutes.
10. Bake in a 400-degree oven for 7 to 10 minutes or just until lightly browned; sprinkle with cinnamon stevia.

Conclusion

Thank you for reading through the Pancreatitis Cookbook. I hope it proved to the ultimate pancreatitis guide and that the pancreatitis diet recipes were able to improve your enzymes and health. Pancreatitis can indeed be a painful disease without the right guidance, so, I hope I was able to provide you with a bit of knowledge to help you through this journey of health.

If you enjoyed what you read through, please consider taking a few minutes to leave me a review on the store on which you purchased this book.

Thanks again!

Made in the USA
Monee, IL
22 October 2024

68470604R00066